Decolonizing Study Abroad through the Identities of Latinx Students

This book counters the common understanding of study abroad in Latin America as a White and middle-class colonizer practice and reimagines it to fit the needs of Latinx immigrant/transnational higher education students.

The book centers Latinx youth inhabiting familial heritage spaces as a pathway toward a deeper understanding of themselves as racialized and colonized individuals, reframing study abroad for Latinx youth as a way for them to reclaim, negotiate, and strengthen their own immigrant/Latino/a/Chicano/a and other identities. The text is undergirded by a theoretical argument based on decolonial methods in education and Critical Race Theory and draws on counter-stories, rich descriptive interviews, and participant observations across 26 years of combined experience leading educational trips to Latin America. The authors analyze, reflect, and critique the field of study abroad to advocate for the rethinking of recruitment strategies, pedagogical experiences, language practices, and community partnerships that include Latino/a, Chicano/a, and Latin American immigrant youth and their families from the beginning. They present a new conceptualization of Latinx immigrant students studying abroad as engaging opportunities for reclaiming heritage, culture, histories, and language, for exploring a sense of identity and obligation to Latin communities, and for healing from the effects of Whiteness and ethnocentrism in ways online possible outside the continental United States. As such, the book shifts the gaze of the entire field toward new diversities showcasing examples of how educational trips abroad can be reenvisioned to suit the needs of ethnically minoritized students in the United States.

This volume will appeal to scholars, researchers, educators, and education officers working across higher education and international education, looking for contemporary, global, and forward-thinking decolonial methodologies.

G. Sue Kasun is Professor of Language Education at the College of Education and Human Development, Georgia State University, USA.

Beth Marks is a faculty member in the Secondary and Middle Grades Education Department at Kennesaw State University, USA.

Julián Jefferies is Associate Professor at California State University, Fullerton, USA.

Routledge Research in Decolonizing Education

The *Routledge Research in Decolonizing Education* series aims to enhance our understanding and facilitate ongoing debates, research, and theory relating to decolonization, decolonizing education and the curriculum, and postcolonialism in education. The series is international in scope and is aimed at upper-level and postgraduate students, researchers, and research students, as well as academics and scholars.

Books in the series include:

Decolonising African University Knowledges, Volume 2
Challenging the Neoliberal Mantra
Edited by Amasa P. Ndofirepi, Felix Maringe, Simon Vurayai, and Gloria Erima

The Patchwork of World History in Texas High Schools
Unpacking Eurocentrism, Imperialism, and Nationalism in the Curriculum, 1920-2021
Stephen Jackson

Exclusionary Rationalities in Brazilian Schooling
Decolonizing Historical Studies
Natália Gil

Funds of Knowledge and Identity Pedagogies for Social Justice
International Perspectives and Praxis from Communities, Classrooms, and Curriculum
Edited by Moisés Esteban-Guitart

Decolonizing Study Abroad through the Identities of Latinx Students
A Manifesto to Reclaim Identities and Heritage
G. Sue Kasun, Beth Marks, and Julián Jefferies

For more information about the series, please visit www.routledge.com/Routledge-Research-in-Decolonizing-Education/book-series/RRDE

Decolonizing Study Abroad through the Identities of Latinx Students
A Manifesto to Reclaim Identities and Heritage

G. Sue Kasun, Beth Marks and Julián Jefferies

NEW YORK AND LONDON

First published 2024
by Routledge
605 Third Avenue, New York, NY 10158

and by Routledge
4 Park Square, Milton Park, Abingdon, Oxon, OX14 4RN

Routledge is an imprint of the Taylor & Francis Group, an informa business

© 2024 G. Sue Kasun, Beth Marks, Julián Jefferies

The right of G. Sue Kasun, Beth Marks and Julián Jefferies to be identified as authors of this work has been asserted in accordance with sections 77 and 78 of the Copyright, Designs and Patents Act 1988.

All rights reserved. No part of this book may be reprinted or reproduced or utilised in any form or by any electronic, mechanical, or other means, now known or hereafter invented, including photocopying and recording, or in any information storage or retrieval system, without permission in writing from the publishers.

Trademark notice: Product or corporate names may be trademarks or registered trademarks, and are used only for identification and explanation without intent to infringe.

ISBN: 978-1-032-33541-4 (hbk)
ISBN: 978-1-032-33542-1 (pbk)
ISBN: 978-1-003-32011-1 (ebk)

DOI: 10.4324/9781003320111

Typeset in Times New Roman
by SPi Technologies India Pvt Ltd (Straive)

Contents

Acknowledgments   vi

Introduction: Why We Need a Manifesto—Study Within as Starting Remedy for Latinx Youth Drowning in U.S. Whiteness   1

1 A Change in Focus: From White Students to Brown Students Abroad   10

2 Decolonizing Study Abroad: Purposeful Design of the Program and Research Approach   28

3 Pedagogical Strategies to Delve Within: A Decolonial Turn toward Renewed Community   49

4 Collaborating with Local Partners and Communities: Through Shared Ownership   69

5 How International Study Creates Opportunities for Personal/Communal Solidarity through Continued Mother Tongue Maintenance, Political Consciousness, and Identity   89

Conclusion: Building the Loving Community— The Manifesto's Promise   105

Index   *115*

Acknowledgments

'Caminante, se hace el camino al andar; journey taker, you make the journey step by step'. This work is possible thanks to the many people who have helped build the programs we have established over the years. For this specific program, we wish to first thank our language and culture school partner of over ten years, CILAC Freire and its director, Martha Mata. Martha has been a tireless advocate of creating loving communities and establishing the necessary structures so they can thrive in the decades she has been doing this work. We also acknowledge her life partner, who has moved on to the next realm, Jorge Torres. His vision inspired the foundation for all this work over 35 years ago, and the same vision has been transformative for individuals the world over, including the first-ever program of Dreamers who were allowed to legally travel from the United States to Mexico to learn about their roots in the mid-2010s.

We also thank the many families and other local grassroots organizations who have fostered our programs and cared deeply about the Latinx students who participated in this program. They have modeled the kind of reciprocity we write about in this text, and we are forever grateful to them.

Georgia State University has allowed this program to run, and we are grateful to all its administrative and academic support over the years, as not all universities recognize the importance of heritage programs or programs that are designed to be decolonial. In particular, Dr. Gertrude Tinker Sachs of Georgia State has been a tireless champion of this vision, and we know the program could not have run without her. Dr. Julián Jefferies would like to thank the Center for Internships and Community Engagement (CICE) at Cal State Fullerton for their support.

Finally, we recognize our families for their support over so many years. These families include the families we were born into, the family members we chose, and the ones we have given life to. They also include the friends who have become family over the years. Marks wants to recognize the inspiration and encouragement from Michael, Jeff, Angel, Greg, and Paige. Kasun thanks her children, Maya and Kai, for the love they have shared for Mexico and its people. Gracias a todos nuestros tan queridos familiares. May we continue planting the seeds of family and loving community in this manifesto and all the work beyond.

Introduction: Why We Need a Manifesto

Study Within as Starting Remedy for Latinx Youth Drowning in U.S. Whiteness

Manifesting Latinx Students as the Center of the Curriculum: Zapata in Morelos, Mexico

In the city center of Cuernavaca, Morelos, the Latinx students stood in front of the statue of Mexican Revolution hero Emiliano Zapata. Some looked with sadness and others with frustration. One of the students cried, 'Why have they hidden this history from us?' In their Eurocentric education in the United States, the students never learned about Indigenous people or cultures in Latin America—it had simply been erased by lack of disclosure. In our education abroad program, the students realized the impact of colonization on their education while they experienced curricular moments centered on Latinx culture and language. This was achieved through activities such as visiting museums and learning about how the state's and country's leading architect of democratic freedom from a dictatorship in the early 1900s became the undergirding vision of collective empowerment over the country, even helping inspire an autonomous communal movement in the far-flung southeastern state of Chiapas 50 years later.

One learning experience that also spun off Zapata's influence was with a charla/testimonial by a local activist supporting the Indigenous movement in Chiapas, Mexico of Zapatismo. Zapatismo is the support of Indigenous communal self-determination based on a communal and truly democratic form of governance that has been incredibly successful since its inception in 1994 and despite government repression (Esteva, 2005; Kasun & Mora-Pablo, 2022). In a written reflection about the charla, Ana explained, 'That's how worth it the cause is'. Learning about Zapata and the Zapatista movement raised the consciousness of the Latinx students in ways of resistance and possibilities for change in marginalized communities. Standing in the city center, Ana realized, 'The history I've been taught in school has truly been irrelevant to my culture, my heritage and the experiences I have lived as a Mexican-American'. Experiencing in person the historical places and culture, the students were free to produce their own knowledge and ideas as they juxtaposed the Western, White-centric discourse they learned in their U.S. schools. Not only were the Latinx students learning history and language skills, but they were also experiencing a sense of belonging/solidaridad and pride. Rewriting history is a form of resistance and agency that the Latinx students learned during the education abroad program as we brought to the forefront their own subjugated history and culture.

***

As transnational scholars in the field of education with years of experience in engaging students in educational travel abroad, we argue for an urgent change in how we think about the field of international education for minoritized Latinx and Chicanx student populations in the United States. Time and time again, we have chosen to return to Latin America with our students as a space within higher education to counter the assimilationist and colonizing forces living among U.S. cultural Whiteness and as a way for them to strengthen their own immigrant/Latinx/Chicanx and other identities. We argue that heritage-seeking educational experiences offer decolonizing possibilities and spaces that are key to their identity construction and healing. We have chosen this particular space because it allows us, even in a short period, a break from our daily lives and family responsibilities, from work, from our daily routines and allows us to isolate ourselves from our performances toward U.S. Whiteness while healing and reclaiming our identities and spaces (Zavala, 2016). We believe that academic experiences that involve travel can be made accessible and possible for Latinx college students by breaking the mold of how travel is usually planned and executed in higher education. For this to happen, we must break away from study abroad as a White and middle-class colonizer practice that engages in voyeurism of the 'Other', reproduces consumerist and individualistic subjectivities and appropriates local cultures (Adkins & Messerly, 2019; Brown, 2005; Said, 1979).

Study abroad programs in U.S. higher education are a direct continuity of the colonial era in that they create and reproduce the Self/Other distinction, constantly look for ways to reproduce Western students as the privileged Self, and look upon Others as needing assistance, help, or cultivation (Adkins & Messerly, 2019). As a mostly White and middle-class student population attend these programs, the literature has looked at how, in the name of 'cultural competence' and individual gains, they venture very little outside of their comfort zone and prefer to carry their 'own homegrown bubble and lifestyle around with them' (Ogden, 2007). White middle-class students, for example, gaze at Cuba from the pool of their air-conditioned hotel (Sharpe, 2015), or dress in sombreros and guaraches in a Mexican 'fiesta' in Mexico City (Ramirez, 2013). In doing so, these kinds of study abroad programs reproduce Western and colonizing ideologies by providing the curriculum in English, privileging individualistic goals over collective ones and exploiting local people and cultures, and reproducing neoliberal practices by producing the student as a consumer-tourist. We engage the notion of neoliberalism in our critique because we see it as a clear extension of postcolonial and neocolonial practices, an economic system which exports individualism, consumption, and personal vs. collective needs as central to perpetuating capitalism. Its outcomes include shifting foci from considering public goods such as education as ways to create cohesion in society toward the project of education becoming the creation of college- and workforce-ready individuals, for instance (Spring, 2018).

There are many critiques from a postcolonial standpoint on how study abroad or education abroad represents a continuation of colonial relations. In most research studies, U.S. White students are traveling abroad. Very little is said about, for example, Latinx students going back to the land of their parents and being able to communicate in Spanish. How does this change how we think about education abroad? For Latinx students, embarking on an educational trip to Latin America is not 'study abroad'. In fact, their experiences of discrimination and treatment as second-class citizens in the United States render them 'abroad at home'. For many of them, returning to Latin America is a way to discover their home, themselves, and their sense of belonging.

We know that the classroom spaces can be a good starting point to counter the forces of assimilation and colonization, and we know that even though the pedagogy that can be employed in the class can be transformative, it is sometimes not enough. In order to offer at transformative pedagogy that helps students to awaken and heal from the daily violences of minoritized students living in White spaces, we need to offer something more. While our students report that they have found respite in Ethnic Studies classes, where they argue 'they can be themselves' or have 'found community', we want to go a step further in describing experiences of powerful experiential pedagogy in the context of education abroad. In this book, we want to argue for the creation of heritage-seeking programs in Latin America as a way to get in contact with the values and ways of being of Latin American cultures, to find a respite from the daily micro-aggressions coming from U.S. cultural Whiteness, and as a way to heal and reclaim their identities (Zavala, 2017).

The added benefit of an educational program away from home, even if it is for a short period of time, is that it allows students to plan for a break from the routine of work, study, and family responsibilities. The orientation of time and space in a capitalist democracy drives students to creatively manage a routine that involves juggling these three in ways that leaves little space for students to reflect on their identity, interests, and goals. By this, we mean that the choice of studying abroad will, in many cases, force students to rethink their orientation to work, the negotiation of responsibilities with their family and their relation of self with their community and social worlds. We have labored to provide students experiences where we facilitate a *diálogo de vivires*, or a 'dialog of livings' wherein students from the United States and the peoples of host countries connect, briefly, about what and how they have lived, even perhaps scratching at a diálogo de saberes (Esteva, 2018; Kasun & Mora-Pablo, 2022). In the case of females, for example, it can force a conversation about gender roles, as our female students frequently negotiate harder restrictions from parents in terms of spending time outside of the home. We have observed a negotiation with their families about ways to organize their family responsibilities while they are away, a conversation about the role of university in their lives and their schooling responsibilities. We have seen how it forces them to negotiate with their bosses, taking days off for an academic field trip, or re-evaluate the job that they are working in, as well as practicing their fundraising and financial planning skills. In sum, short trips outside of their geographical zone offer a rupture of their daily lives, force a conversation with family, and create a reevaluation of college, work, and family responsibility balances. We have found that this rupture can be transformative for Latinx college students in a positive way.

Pedagogically, heritage-seeking programs abroad offer us the possibility to have the undivided attention of students for a significant period of time and their own space for reflection on very different terms than what can occur within the United States. This is not possible in the busy daily routine of immigrant college students, who find it hard to participate in college fully because of family responsibilities, work, and the feeling that they do not belong on campus. We have found that the economic reality of immigrant families dictates that they work, sometimes more than one job, while attending school while at the same time attempting to avoid loans at all costs, a cultural aversion to debt that in reality seems to be little understood in education practices. Added to the family responsibilities that many of them are required to perform at home, it is difficult for students to attend the needed counseling sessions with career professionals, or participate in internships, or get involved in college groups. We have found that an effective approach to short-term programs includes careful financial planning, targeted mentoring, career counseling, and the involvement of the family. This can be transformative for students to break out of routines of jobs that are not related to their discipline, can transform the kind of support they receive from their families for college and graduate school, and can transform their identity in terms of resisting the negative forces of assimilation in U.S. society.

Introduction: Why We Need a Manifesto   5

The U.S. context in which Latinx live in, on a daily basis, devalues their culture, discriminates against them, pressures them to assimilate to U.S. cultural Whiteness, to act White, and to interact in spaces that 'de-culturalize' them, their language, and community (Valenzuela, 1999). They attend schools where the value of Spanish is not only disregarded but seen as a sign of their limited proficiency in English (Gándara & Contreras, 2010). They watch, listen, and interact with media that portrays their culture as 'illegal', as violent, or as subservient (Picker & Chyng, 2013). On a daily basis, our students fear being deported or a family member being deported (De Genova, 2004) as immigration enforcement focuses on detention and removal of immigrants as a way to purportedly deal with the issue. This even manifests into daily guilt and is carried with them into study abroad spaces (Kaneria, Kasun, & Marks, 2022). This context pressures students to navigate their home and work/school identity in complicated and resourceful ways, with students resorting to different tactics in order to adapt and protect themselves. Some of them resort to dressing in a more 'White' way in order to fit in and survive, and some choose not to speak in Spanish in certain spaces in order to develop a strong 'White' native accent in order to pass by. A decolonizing pedagogical program that argues for a return to Latin America and the construction of a 'space without White people' serves as a starting point for a place to heal and recover from these daily violences.

A Space 'Without White People': Healing, Reclaiming

We work and study in a majority of White spaces. For people of color, being in these spaces is 'like being an actor onstage. There are roles one has to perform, storylines one is expected to follow and subplots one should avoid at all costs', as Carbado and Gulatti (2013, p. 1) so aptly describe. In their observations of African Americans in predominantly White institutions, survival means that they are expected to act White enough to keep their jobs but also Black enough for the few co-workers of the same race. Honing in on what many people of color's performance look like at work or at school, they describe 'Working Identity' as the 'ways of being, including how one dresses, speaks, styles one's hair; one's politics and view about race' (p. 1) that are a part of our performance. Whether we choose silence over a White peer's racist comment, or we accept a wrong Anglicized pronunciation of our names, or try to dress more professionally than our bosses to make up for our outsider status, people of color engage in performance in White spaces that distance ourselves from our cultural selves.

Even though we would like to think that the university offers a space that shields students from the daily violences of being Latinx, both the literature and student testimonies tell us that they face many of the same issues at the university. Racial and cultural microaggressions are common, and students report that they change who they really are in order to please the professor and get better grades. This is why we argue that for education to be truly decolonizing for Latinx college students, it needs to involve spaces 'without White people' (Blackwell, 2018). Facilitator and coach Kelsey Blackwell explains well the fact that people of color can find healing and a connection to their authentic selves in these spaces. Around White people, there is a tendency to act according to White cultural norms and behaviors, to muzzle our own voices and ways of being in order to make them more comfortable. She argues that '[i]n integrated spaces, patterns of white dominance are inevitable' (Blackwell, 2018, p. 3):

> The values of whiteness are the water in which we all swim. No one is immune. Those values dictate who speaks, how loud, when, the words we use, what we don't say, what is ignored, who is validated and who is not. Unless we are actively and persistently dismantling these constructs, we are abiding by them. In integrated spaces (where we are less likely to be ourselves given the divisions that white dominance has created), we fall into the roles society has assigned us. As a person of color, and perhaps the only one in the room, it's exhausting to always be swimming upstream.
>
> (p. 5)

As it plays out in classroom spaces, students of color will act differently when they are in a class with White students as opposed to all students of color. Short-term educational trips abroad can help Latinx students step away from U.S. Whiteness in order to name, analyze, and acknowledge its consequences in our daily lives.

Complexities of Who We Take and with Whom We Work

Are we, in fact, arguing for segregation in our education abroad trips in order to give space for Latinx students to have a space 'outside of Whiteness' and heal from its deleterious effects? Yes, we are. We acknowledge, however, that this does not come without its difficulties in implementation. We acknowledge that in the supposed 'post-race' environment we live in we are in danger of being called out 'racist' or discriminatory because we do not want to involve White students in our educational programs. We find it difficult, also, to recruit enough students of color in our programs and thus have to open up enrollment to all ethnicities, complicating the goal of providing a 'space outside of Whiteness'. We understand that Latin America is not a space that is devoid of Whiteness and *blanqueamiento* (Telles & Flores, 2013), of course, and that colorism still exists in the places that we visit. Most important of all, we acknowledge that our students and us have internalized notions of White supremacy in many ways and forms and we may have lost our Spanish and Indigenous languages in the process of colonization, making it hard to convince students of the urgency and necessity of these kinds of educational experiences.

In the midst of these challenges, the issue of language proficiency is an important one: we have to decide whether we ask for students to have at least an intermediate level of Spanish fluency, understanding that when we take English monolingual students to Latin America we are in some ways reifying notions of American exceptionalism and the hegemony of English while at the same time nurturing students' linguistic comfort zone. At the same time, we are conscious that many of our Latinx students have experienced language loss due to no fault of their own, as entrenched structural issues have discouraged them or not given them an opportunity to maintain their home language. As such, we generally lean to the side of accommodating for less Spanish so as not to preclude access to any students who want to attend.

Acknowledging the fact that this work is messy, we continue to see a return to Latin America as a 'situated pedagogical practice' (Zavala, 2016) that helps students not only *name* their social worlds but also, importantly, *heal* from the effects of colonialism in their lives. Zavala (2016) pays attention to the role of healing in decolonial methodologies, arguing that 'because colonialism deculturizes people and separates them from who they are, their communities, practices, languages and land, there is ample room and need for healing as a strategy for community self-determination' (p. 4). In this vein, we call for a return to Latin America as a space for Latinx students to recover from the physical, cultural, social, and psychological trauma experienced in the United States and at the same time reconnecting with each other and Mother Earth (Zavala, 2016). We believe strongly, based on our research (e.g. Kasun et al., 2020) and our many experiences, that an educational trip in Latin America can provide the space for this to happen. This book is a testimony to that.

Overview of the Book

In the first chapter, we make the case for a change in positionality when thinking about creating educational programs abroad for Latinx students and other students of color, offering alternative theoretical orientations. In Chapter 2, we delve into the purposeful conception and design of a program that does not reproduce the 'students as tourists' paradigm while instead creating a space for students to reengage their birth rights to their cultures and heritages. Giving concrete examples from a program in Cuernavaca, Mexico, we describe how faculty and coordinators need a certain degree of flexibility in how to recruit students, plan activities, choose a location, create partnerships, decide where students will room and eat, find collaborative partners, and deal with third-party providers. Chapter 3 reimagines pedagogical activities in heritage programs. One example of a decolonial pedagogical strategy featured is relationship building, describing how the learning that occurred in both structured and spontaneous experiences during the study abroad program was impactful due to the relational component.

An important part of developing decolonial approaches to education abroad has to do with the always-unequal relationship developed with local partners. In Chapter 4, we focus on this key issue, recognizing the power dynamics of working in spaces that are less resourced than the 50 U.S. states where we reside and exploring our efforts of creating dialogic and caring relationships with our host partners on site. Chapter 5 gives a detailed description of student experiences as evidence of feeling newly included in community—linguistically and racially. We give ethnographic detail on how Latinx students reconnected within in ways that empowered them and transformed their feelings of cultural marginalization with the ability to carry forward a personal identity toolkit upon return to the Whitely hostile U.S. terrain.

In the conclusion, we return to the importance of changing the frame of how we see 'study abroad' in educational institutions in the United States as we dare to dream our programs into life. As the United States becomes increasingly Brown and otherwise diverse, it is increasingly reckoning with demographic shifts—even if for little other reason than market pressures that recognize the buying power of Brown communities. We also provide words of caution about how to avoid pitfalls we and close providers in Mexico have experienced regarding critically oriented international study experiences. Beyond a sense of marketizing Brown dollars that could be thrown at study abroad, we instead draw from the threads of strengths these communities have brought to what is now U.S. soil toward reclaiming strengths for cultural and communal maintenance. We revisit the highlights shared in preceding chapters and synthesize lessons by providing a set of recommendations and guiding principles. This is all toward helping build small, loving communities in these programs who can sow seeds upon return of the loving communities they experience during their programs.

References

Adkins, R. & Messerly, B. (2019). Toward decolonizing education abroad: Moving beyond the self/other dichotomy. In E. Brewer & A. Ogden (Eds.), *Critical perspectives on integrating education abroad into undergraduate education*. Stylus Publishing, LLC, Sterling, VA.

Blackwell, K. (2018). Why people of color need spaces without white people. *The Arrow*, open access.

Introduction: Why We Need a Manifesto 9

Brown, A. L. (2005). The "other:" examining the "other" in education. In S. J. Farenga, B. A. Joyce & D. Ness (Eds.), *Encyclopedia on education and human development* (Armonk, N. Y. ed., pp. 289–292) M.E. Sharpe.

Carbado, D & Gulatti, M (2013). *Acting White? Rethinking Race in Post-Racial America*. New York: Oxford University Press.

De Genova, N. (2004). The Legal Production of Mexican/Migrant "Illegality". *Latino Studies 2*, 160–185. https://doi.org/10.1057/palgrave.lst.8600085

Esteva, G. (2018). Figueroa "Más allá de la tormenta", Revista CoPaLa. Año 3, número 6, julio-diciembre 2018. pp. 7–27. ISSN: 2500-8870. Disponible en: http://www.revistacopala.co

Esteva, G. (2005). Celebration of Zapatismo. *Humboldt Journal of Social Relations*, 29(1), 127–167.

Gándara, P., & Contreras, F. (2010). *The Latino education crisis: The consequences of failed social policies*. United Kingdom: Harvard University Press.

Kaneria, A. J., Kasun, G. S., & Marks, B. W. (2022). "Why Am I the One Who Gets to Go to Mexico?": Nepantlera Bridging Among Latinx Students in a Decolonial Study Abroad Program. *Teachers College Record*, 124(9), 122–148. https://doi.org/10.1177/01614681221132942

Kasun, G.S., & Mora-Pablo, I. (2022). Conclusion. In G.S. Kasun & I. Mora-Pablo (Eds.), *Applying Anzalduan frameworks to understand transnational youth identities: Bridging culture, language, and schooling at the U.S.-Mexico border*. New York: Routledge, 173–178.

Kasun, G.S., Hernández, T., & Montiel, H. (2020). The engagement of transnationals in Mexican university classrooms: Points of entry towards recognition among future English teachers. *Multicultural Perspectives*, 22(1), 37–45. https://doi.org/10.1080/15210960.2020.1728273

Ogden, A. (2007). The view from the Veranda: Understanding today's colonial student. *Frontiers: The Interdisciplinary Journal of Study Abroad*, 5(1).

Picker, M., & Chyng, S. (2013). Latinos Beyond Reel: Challenging a Media Stereotype. https://latinosbeyondreel.com/

Ramirez, G. B. (2013). Learning abroad or just going abroad. International education in opposite sides of the border. *The Qualitative Report*, 18(31), 1–11. Retrieved from https://nsuworks.nova.edu/tqr/vol18/iss31/2

Said, E. (1979). *Orientalism*. New York: Vintage Books.

Sharpe, E. (2015). Colonialist tendencies in education abroad. *International Journal of Teaching and Learning in Higher Education*, 27(2), 227–234.

Spring, J. (2018). *American education* 18th ed.. New York: Routledge.

Telles, E., & Flores, R. (2013). Not just color: Whiteness, nation, and status in Latin America. *Hispanic American Historical Review*, 93(3), 411–449.

Valenzuela, A. (1999). *Subtractive schooling: U.S. - Mexican Youth and the politics of caring*. New York: State University of New York Press.

Zavala, M. (2016). Design, participation, and social change: What design in grassroots spaces can teach learning scientists. *Cognition & Instruction* 34(3), 236–249.

Zavala, M. (2017). Decolonial methodologies in education. In: M. Peters (Eds.), *Encyclopedia of educational philosophy and theory*. Springer, Singapore. https://doi.org/10.1007/978-981-287-532-7_498-1

1 A Change in Focus

From White Students to Brown Students Abroad

In this chapter, we argue for a change in how we imagine spaces when thinking about creating educational programs abroad for Latinx students and other students of color. Throughout this chapter, we offer an alternative theoretical orientation to reenvision study abroad programs in higher education in order to oppose a direct continuity of the colonial era which creates and reproduces the Self/Other distinction, constantly looks for ways to reproduce Western students as the privileged Self, and looks upon Others as needing assistance, help, or cultivation (Adkins & Messerly, 2019).

We have to reimagine what education abroad looks like for a population that is 'othered' in the spaces in which the 'other' inhabits, studies, and works. This is why we argue that for education to be truly decolonizing for Latinx college students, it needs to involve spaces 'without White people' and raise consciousness (Blackwell, 2018; Mohanty, 2003). Blackwell (2018) explains well the fact that people of color can find healing and a connection to their authentic selves in these spaces. Conversely, she notes, that while students of color are around White people, there is a tendency to act according to White cultural norms and behaviors, to muzzle their own voices and ways of being in order to make them more comfortable (2018). Blackwell argues that '[i]n integrated spaces, patterns of white dominance are inevitable' (2018, p. 3). In this chapter, we foreground the how of avoiding these pitfalls and working towards healing.

The chapter delves into reimagining an educational program in Mexico that isolated Latinx students, for a short period of time, from Whiteness in order to allow for a deeper reclaiming of their identities, culture, and families, as well as allow for healing to take place (Zavala, 2016) (even with a very limited number of White people participating but through an engaged consciousness that allows ideological space for non-Whiteness). Healing was an act of replacing feelings of self-doubt manifested through marginalization in the United States with self-compassion as the group collectively shared personal stories of oppression. We review the literature on decolonial approaches to education and to study abroad and use auto-ethnographic and interview data to illustrate these important theoretical underpinnings. We now turn our attention to the notion of what it means to decolonize study abroad.

Turning the Focus toward Students of Color in Education Abroad

Considering all the study abroad students from the United States, only 28% of the students identify as non-White, although the numbers of non-White students has been increasing over the past decade (IIE, 2019). According to the U.S. National Center for Education Statistics (NCES), undergraduate students of color in U.S. postsecondary institutions was 44.2% in 2018 (Latinx 20.5%, Black 12.6%, Asian 6.6%, mixed race 3%, and Native American/Pacific Islander 1.5%). The majority of U.S. study abroad students are White and female (White: 70%, Female: 67%). Students of color comprise 30% of U.S. study abroad students in comparison to their overall representation in postsecondary education of 44.2%, as mentioned above. It's worth stating the obvious; there is a disparity in study abroad representation that merits consideration and remedying where possible.

Studies of students of color in study abroad specify the benefits for marginalized students related to self-actualization (Willis, 2015), agency and empowerment (Chang, 2017; Wick et al., 2019), and resistant capital (Hartman et al., 2020) as they relate to ways marginalized communities resist the messages of the dominant culture to delegitimize and erase cultural meanings they value by consciously conveying messages and behaviors that challenge the status quo (McLaren, 2015; Yosso, 2005).

The actual act of studying abroad involves a relational approach between the students and the local host community. As students of color travel from the Global North to the Global South, the interactions and cultural self-reflections become more complicated. For instance, critical investigations of power hierarchies and relations within study abroad and teacher education (and beyond) immersions need to be researched (Doerr, 2015; Smolcic & Katunich, 2017). Critical future research needs to focus on the study abroad student's cultural background, racial and gendered identities, and the student's motives for participating in a study abroad program (Smolcic & Katunich, 2017). These studies could help illuminate pathways toward increasing the participation of students of color in study abroad.

Student Decision to Study in Latin America: Ancestral Homelands

Students seeking education abroad experiences in ancestral homelands often have feelings and thoughts about traveling where they perceive a familiar place, although realities may vary from expectations. Research on students of color who are 'going home' describe the students feeling a sense of connection to the people and place of the host community during the study abroad program. Often described in the research as *heritage destinations* (Rubin, 2004; Wick et al., 2019), these are locations for study abroad students that reflect their heritage (e.g. U.S. Latinx students studying in Latin America and U.S. Asian students studying in Asia). The literature indicates that heritage-seeking students find education abroad programs in heritage locations contribute to positive identity development (Raymondi, 2005) and to gains in confidence (Guerrero, 2006). Students studying in ancestral homelands demonstrate a strong desire to gain a deeper understanding of their own cultural identity and better understand their own family (Rubin, 2004). To counteract the lack of family support for students of color to study abroad and leave home, heritage destinations tend to prompt positive family responses (Nguyen, 2014). Family support for study abroad is greater when the family members feel they have insight and knowledge concerning a place (Nguyen, 2014). For example, family members of Latinx students often encourage them to study abroad in Latin America to increase an understanding of cultural heritage and gain language skills. Students go to these homelands to construct their own impressions beyond their family's images shaped by their own lived experiences.

In one study, Wick et al. (2019) explored community cultural wealth (CCW) with several heritage-seeking social work students in Costa Rica. The findings indicate that students leveraged linguistic and familial capital during the program. The students felt connected to their *Tico* (familial term for native Costa Ricans)/host families because of language skills and shared cultural references. These commonalities were used by the students to connect with the host community. In participant Quetzali's journal, she reflects:

> My ethnic background [Mexican] has assisted me in having a better understanding of how and why do people in Costa Rica behave in a certain way. For instance, my homestay mother is very religious and I feel that my religious background [and] being Mexican has definitely assisted me in building a strong connection with her.
>
> (p. 72)

The connection felt between Quetzali and her host mother is due to lived experiences they share. Students connect and learn with the capacity for empathy, in order to gain a deeper understanding of the host community while they also acknowledge the differences within cultural groups (Belenky et al., 1986). Another student explains her experiences and connection to the host community:

> So it just made me reflect a little bit on how maybe their experiences are similar with family members that have also come to the United States and have integrated and have assimilated into the culture as well.

> So it just made me [also] realize that the different levels of experiences that we had even within the same ethnicity or race can make us be very different or identify very differently based on our experiences.
>
> (Wick et al., 2019, p. 72)

This student is aware of feeling connected to cultural commonalities while being interdependent at the same time (Keating, 2013). Her comments express border thinking as her gaze on the United States is altered. She reflects on her cultural heritage connection in Costa Rica and her family members who immigrated to the United States and adopted the dominant culture (Mignolo, 2011). The student interactions in the host country highlight the complexities of identities.

Students studying in ancestral lands navigate complex emotions and situations through the intersectionality of their identities. In some instances, the student may experience the 'real' local culture as local communities consider the students part of the community due to their language and/or ethnic identities. Some U.S. students of color feel dissonance when they do not experience connection to the host community because they are perceived as 'American' without ethnic ties in the host country (Willis, 2015). Other students may experience alienation from the local community as they consider the students too 'American' (Willis, 2015). Study abroad programs can support students of color as they navigate their identity by creating spaces to initiate dialogue about reactions and experiences before, during, and after the program related to the intersections of their sometimes-hidden identities with the host country.

The literature on students of color in study abroad programs suggests the experiences and connections are unique in heritage destinations and other places where cultural relevance is leveraged (Chang, 2017; Wick et al., 2019). Study abroad faculty can increase interest by developing programs in places where students of color make a connection to their own ethnic background and students develop a relational worldview of interconnectedness as they interact and create relations with the people and place of the host country.

The findings in these studies recommend study abroad programs to be cognizant of the social composition of study abroad programs improving the access and quality for underrepresented students (Blake et al., 2020; Chang, 2017; Hartman et al., 2020; Wick et al., 2019; Willis, 2015). Pedagogically, study abroad programs identify culturally validating experiences for students of color and prepare students for issues that may arise during the program, which underscores the connectedness of the students between themselves and the host community (Chang, 2017; Willis, 2015). In a study abroad program, students understand a relational worldview when they also know the history of the people in the place.

Decolonizing Study Abroad

Study abroad and immersive experiences have historically been structured through a lens of coloniality, promoting a binary logic that divides people into Euro-Western and Other. For all involved in the experiences, it then invites comparisons about the norms of the host country, which are then often interpreted as inferior, exotic, 'quaint', and so on. What we long to avoid are the arms of White students ending in a finger pointing at the quaint/curious/odd 'Other' who may be drinking something differently, squatting differently, or wearing clothing differently than what the White gaze is used to. Such gazing is perpetuated in study abroad student communal meals, tourism with little regard for locals' feelings about the study abroad student visitors, and so on.

We thus name this often-unspoken lens of coloniality as a starting point toward the relational ideology of decolonization as a remedy to the problems of study abroad. We locate the geopolitics of the Global North and Global South as an alternative analytic to the concept of globalization, which homogenizes societies and cultures. The Global South refers to regions outside of Europe and North America and the thinking and being that comes from the peoples of these places. According to the Manitoba Council for International Cooperation (2020), the terminology 'Global South was chosen by the people living in places like the Caribbean, Latin America, South America, Africa, and part of Asia to describe themselves' (p. vi). De Sousa Santos (2016) refers to the Global South as people and places that are excluded or marginalized by capitalism. Through his writings, de Sousa Santos emphasizes the Global South as a distinct place of intellectual production and epistemologies. Relations between the Global North and Global South are not only global but also local. Gloria Anzaldúa (1987) explained the borderlands as a place where colonialism exists within the boundaries of North America. Borderlands represent marginalized people within the boundaries of the Global North. In the United States, the dynamics of the Global North and Global South are seen in the historical and political context of Indigenous people and lands (Battiste, 2000; Pirbhai-Illich & Martin, 2019).

Researchers use the lenses of decolonization to analyze the construction and hierarchy of race and racism established by colonialism, among other forms of oppression such as unbridled capitalism. To 'unsettle' the hierarchy of race, a new description of how we define being human needs to be established outside of colonial discourse (Wynter, 2003). The agenda of decolonization is a strategic response to the colonial process without seeking a single answer but allowing for multiple ways to overcome colonialism (Grande, 2015). Some of the goals people try to achieve through decolonization include a shared culture within a community and a coexistence through diversity (languages, ways of knowing, worldviews)

(Grande, 2015; Mignolo, 2011). Global relations have been impacted through the historical, economic, and sociopolitical aspects of colonialism creating struggles and assertions of power and privilege. Linda Tuhiwai Smith (2013) describes the related notion of postcolonialism from an Indigenous perspective: she notes in this vein of thinking, colonization has been dissolved and does not exist because the colonizers have left. Postcolonialism is a process to expel the colonizer and remove colonial power, which has not fully occurred (Grande, 2015; Smith, 2013). Indigenous people are still seeking justice from the Global North in this configuration. According to Smith, the concept of decolonization, however, is a process of 'divesting of colonial power', which is different than postcolonialism. To disrupt the discourse of colonization, Indigenous people often express their history and their stories about their communities instead of letting others define them. The phrase 'cognitive imperialism' describes the way Eurocentric ideologies dominate the mind because of forced assimilation (Battiste, 2000). Indigenous communities expressing their culture, language, and social practices is part of the process of decolonization.

Scholars focusing on decolonization make clear that decolonization and colonialism are not binary (Grande, 2015; Mignolo, 2011; Quijano, 2000). Indeed, several Latin American theorists have defined the notion of coloniality as a continuation of the formal project of colonization but that is more cultural and less about the overt power-grabbing of the nation state. Coloniality is the continuation of the imbalance in global power relations and the acknowledgment that colonialism takes many forms (Mignolo, 2011; Quijano, 2000; Walsh, 2007). Within the coloniality framework, the West's project of colonization ended during the 21st century, although the Westernization of the world continues through neoliberalism and other forms of oppression. The sociocultural power dynamic between European and non-European still exists as the legacy of colonialism. At the same time, land remains a key piece of sense-making related to decoloniality, Indigeneity, and who belongs where.

Understanding Land and Settler Colonialism

Settler colonialism is described by Tuck, McKenzie, and McCoy (2014) as a form of colonization where outsiders take over land inhabited by Indigenous peoples and claim it as their own. The settlers position themselves as superior to the 'wild' people that need to be 'tamed'. Indigenous peoples are forced from their land through treaties, violence, and disease. The treaties were signed in good faith by Indigenous people and broken by the government in power (Battiste, 2000). Land-based settlement occurs as settlers need more space and then claim ownership through personal property. Settlers gain resources and make the land their own with the support of the government (Tuck & Yang, 2012). The destruction of Indigenous communities and their connection to place began as soon as Europeans settled in the Americas. Land and its environs are living entities and not commodities to be bought, sold, mined, stripped, and exploited. The Western idea of land as renewable and sustainable is different than land as a home and cultural identity (Kimmerer, 2013). Grande (2015) writes about how these laws of the land create an environment for people, plants, animals, and minerals to thrive and flourish through reciprocity. Reciprocity allows for land and water to be a source for life and, in return, people give gratitude and care for the world. Indigenous communities maintain resources and continuity of place through a right relationship with the land. Being in a right relationship with the land is an Indigenous way to live in a sustainable, loving relationship with all of nature (Kimmerer, 2013). If people take care of the land, the land will care for all living things. Settler colonialism disrupts the Indigenous community's relationship with the land as Indigenous people are forcibly removed from the land (Tuck & Yang, 2012). For Tuck and Yang (2012), the only way forward through decolonization is with land reparations.

Pirbhai-Illich and Martin (2019), scholars with a history of considering immersive study abroad experiences, have a different view about settler colonialism and believe the future is through an understanding of 'how different ways of being and knowing produce different relationships with land' (p. 87). Indigenous ways of knowing and their views of the world are shaped by living intimately with the land (Battiste, 2013). Pirbhai-Illich and Martin (2019) critique the lack of literature on North to South immersion programs and study abroad programs in relation to the colonial aspects of the land. This book is one effort to highlight a North to South immersion program with the notion of decoloniality and students of Global South heritage at the center of the text. This heritage also includes knowledge and ways of knowing that have resisted, to some extents, the imposition of Westernization and pressures of the Global North, an area to which we now turn.

Decolonization of Western Ways of Knowing

Latin American theorists Quijano and Mignolo noted that colonialism has not ended and continues through the ideology of coloniality (Mignolo, 2011; Quijano, 2000). Coloniality privileges the Eurocentric way of being and knowing as 'normal' and any variations as 'other'. Coloniality, as a way of knowing, is founded on a hierarchal structure. Decolonization, as an alternative way of knowing, concentrates on a relational structure.

Boaventura de Sousa Santos (2016) claims that Western thought through a Westernized epistemology has dominated the colonized at the expense of the epistemology of marginalized people with their local knowledge and wisdom. Western Eurocentric ways of thinking are considered superior, making this way of thinking prominent across the Global North and Global South. European texts, histories, concepts, and values dominate across the Global North and the Global South (Cortina et al., 2019; Mitchell, 2019). The failure to recognize how people in the Global South understand their daily life experiences and acknowledge what they value through varied ways of knowing is called cognitive injustice (Mitchell, 2019; Santos, 2016). Western ideology colonizes the 'other' by reducing their pluriverse of diverse ways of knowing and learning into one universal system (Prakash & Esteva, 1998).

The acceptance and coexistence of different ways of knowing are based on decoloniality. Gustavo Esteva (2018) explains, 'if we want to seriously take into consideration different ways of knowing, we need to consider at least four different elements' (p. 502): First, there is an understanding of what counts as knowledge. Second, how knowledge is shared and received is known. Third, power and politics play a role in the relationships between members of the community, and the fourth element considers how the knowledge is used in the community (Esteva, 2018). Indigenous people do not have one way of knowing but acknowledge a pluriverse view of the world with many ways of understanding the world (Four Arrows, 2016; Mignolo, 2011). Four Arrows (2016) notes that the concept of *worldview* is a Western construct and may not fully explain the vision and understanding of Indigenous people.

Framing Implications for Heritage Programs

Even though the political condition of colonialism ended, coloniality continues the European and non-European sociocultural hierarchy through politics, economics, and culture (Quijano, 2000). According to Anibal Quijano (2000), the 'idea of race' [an invented construct with real material consequences] was a tool invented 500 years ago and used by the colonizer to socially dominate the colonized. Within the Latin American region, a human hierarchy of castes was created among Spaniards, Indigenous peoples, and enslaved peoples, based on perceived race. To unsettle coloniality, a (re)definition and (re)description of humans and race needs to be created (Walsh, 2007). As the paths between North America and Latin America diverge, North America creates itself as superior through global capitalism (Walsh, 2007). This creates an us/them dynamic within a Latin American country and also between Global North and Global South countries. Clearly, study abroad can be an easy tool of continued coloniality in terms of who gets to visit whom and under what conditions, with whose resources. It almost goes without saying that these visits are one-way tickets of Global North to Global South. With these conditions of the materially resourced, the question then becomes, how does one devise a study abroad that can be decolonial? That is our project and the work of this book—to show how we attempted to (and in many ways succeeded to) subvert these power dynamics toward a decolonial effort of healing.

Immersion programs need to reduce the risk of continued oppression for people who are marginalized by coloniality (Pirbhai-Illich & Martin, 2019). The authors suggest teacher educators decolonize themselves by accepting coloniality as a global system and for teacher educators who are White to educate themselves. Teacher educators who embody Whiteness need to expand their thinking to include other ways of knowing and, also, learn how to disconnect from structures that privilege them. In immersion programs, teacher educators decolonize themselves and the program by considering the geopolitics of places.

The lived experience of students is unique and place-specific, which is based on the context of the history and geopolitics of where they live. Because classrooms are spaces where difference exists, immersion programs are used by educational institutions to develop intercultural competencies (Pirbhai-Illich et al., 2017). Pirbhai-Illich and Martin (2019) analyze international immersion and service learning programs in teacher education in *Decolonizing Teacher Education in Immersion Contexts: Working with Space, Place, and Boundaries*. Their analysis focuses on students from the Global North participating in a teacher preparation immersion program located in the Global South to prepare them for culturally and linguistically diverse classrooms. To be clear, the authors identify education experiences in the Global South as both global and local such as First Nations schools in Canada. According to the authors, there is a lack of evidence of the transferability of intercultural competencies into the classroom which can be explained by students reverting to the colonial discourse of feeling threatened by changes to a national culture once they are home/Global North. Another consideration for Global North–Global South immersion programs is the assumption by students that they understand a culture through proximity. Without confronting their own positionality, students are unable to disrupt their own views on the sociocultural and historical contexts that they come from.

In *A decolonizing study abroad program in Mexico for pre-service teachers: Taking on the cultural mismatch between Teachers and Students*, Kasun (2017) analyzes a teacher education study abroad program from the Global North to the Global South (Mexico) using a decolonizing lens. The ways the study abroad program demonstrated decolonizing approaches was by including Indigenous ways of knowing in the curriculum through readings and experiences, building mutual relationships with partners in Mexico, and creating a sense of community among the study abroad students. The place, the community, and the students were interconnected in the learning experience. 'Decolonization also refers to the need to understand the histories of systemic oppression and efforts to thrive in the collective by responding in ways that lead toward recognition of past/present histories of oppression and toward our collective healing' (Kasun, 2017, p. 192). The preservice teachers' empathy generated by the study abroad program for migrants in the United States demonstrates the connectivity in this study abroad program. The program also expresses decolonization with the study abroad students' acknowledgment that different ways of knowing can coexist.

One foundational way to resist colonization and achieve aspects of the decolonial is through language claiming and reclamation. This objective becomes possible when centering Latinx (or other historically marginalized raciolinguistic groups) as the protagonists of an international study program. Rather than follow the historic template of providing rich language learning immersion experiences for assumed White students to learn a new *skill*, the design of study abroad for heritage speakers to have access to a heritage language foregrounds part of their identities—in this case, linguistic. Indeed, study abroad has almost always studied second language, White students learning a new language, not people who are enhancing their heritage language skills (Marijuan & Sanz, 2018). We echo the call by Marqués-Pascual (2021) to decolonize programming for heritage Spanish speakers by centering their linguistic identities and providing agentic spaces for them to enact their language heritages.

Shively (2016, 2018) has examined much of the emerging (and still limited) literature related to heritage speakers of other languages on what she calls study abroad. Her reviews indicate that heritage speakers learn more of the target language when they grew up speaking the language to some extent and/or made visits to the home country as children. She explains they may encounter racialized negative experiences based on skin color and physical aspects, with the host country residents having higher expectations of their insider knowledge and/or whether they get 'special' treatment as visitors or not. In a more recent review, Burgo (2020) adds that instructors of heritage speakers in the receiving context should have special guidance about how to meet the specific backgrounds heritage seekers bring linguistically and culturally. She also suggests that service learning be added as a component of programs she argues should be carefully tailored. Kaneria, Kasun, and Marks (2022) explain that through a carefully tailored program with heritage learners in mind, the students were able to develop a rich understanding of 'home' as being pan-national and one that builds on their language backgrounds while developing an increasing sociopolitical consciousness about global factors creating immigration movements. Clearly, there needs to be additional work that centers Latinx heritage seekers, the very heart of what this book has centered.

20 *A Change in Focus*

We turn now to the nine Latinx study abroad participants in this study, a constellation of Latinxs of varying ages, immigration histories, and linguistic and national backgrounds. Like all people, each of the students was complex and at times difficult, but, more often than not, we were able to create a group wherein our strengths shone through. Below we offer highlights of these strengths and creativities of the students in the program.

Student Participants

The students in the study abroad program were enrolled in a large urban college in the Southeast. Student participants in the study abroad program included five graduate students, including Marks (who was a doctoral student at the time), and eight undergraduate students. All the students in the study abroad program consented to the study, although we selected the nine Latinx students as the focus of this study (Marks, 2022). Six of the Latinx students were part of a Latinx outreach program within

Figure 1.1 Participant hands. Photo by Sue Kasun, author.

the college and were traditional-aged undergraduate students. This Latinx outreach program provided mentors and scholarships for undergraduate students of Latinx heritage and provided scholarships and two mentors to accompany the Latinx students on the study abroad program.

Eva (all names are pseudonyms). Eva was a graduate student in education who considered herself Latina. She had worked for two large school systems in the United States with a compassionate approach to doing parent and community outreach among the Latinx community in both districts. Such work seemed natural to her based on her deep knowledge of Latinx communities spanning borders as well as her warmth. A great deal of her community empathy originated from the working-class background of her youth. She was currently living in Mexico with her husband and two young children. Originally, she and her husband were from Colombia and moved to the United States for school, where they lived for 20 years. Her husband worked for a large corporation, and she had worked in Latinx family outreach in the United States. Recently, she had moved with her husband and two children to Mexico and met us at the airport in Mexico City to begin the study abroad program.

Silvia. At the beginning of the program, Silvia was concerned about connecting with the participants because she was seven or more years older than the undergraduate students and younger than the graduate students. Silvia had a gift of deep introspection and was also careful about how often she expressed herself. She identified as Mexican-American and Chicana as well as bisexual. She was completing a master's in social work with an aim of helping the Latinx community. After our second class where she believed all the participants were open and vulnerable, she felt the boundary of age was crossed by connecting. She expressed herself during the program as a feminist and Latina or Hispanic. A second-generation immigrant, she had roots and family in Mexico.

Lupe. Lupe was an undergraduate student with a passion for politics and was part of the outreach program with scholarship. She self-identified as a bisexual Chicana, with Chicana being a fairly unusual term at the time in the Southeastern United States. In class, she discussed the undocumented status (without legal documentation to be in the country) in the United States of her immigrant parents who journeyed from Mexico. The experience of being in Mexico released feelings of guilt for Lupe because she was able to cross the border and travel to Mexico while her parents could not. The sacrifices of her family were made clear as she disclosed that her father was unable to attend his father's (Lupe's grandfather) funeral.

Ana. Ana was completing her degree in teacher education, an undergraduate at the time. From the beginning of the program, she was willing to meet new people as she mentioned that she knew nobody when she signed up for the study abroad program. Ana allowed us to call her by her first name, not the second more Anglicized name her mother had strategically crafted for her (something like 'Susan' in lieu of 'Susana'). As we discussed decolonization during the first pre-departure meeting, she and Kasun considered her use of 'Ana'. She said, 'Yeah, let's go with that this time'. She eagerly built relationships across age, sexuality, and ethnicity and was deeply curious about all the course material and experiences, exhibiting a high level of sophistication at weaving decolonial theory to the course experiences. During the program, she struggled with feelings of guilt and joy as she was able to travel to Mexico and immerse herself in the culture while her undocumented parents could not return to Mexico.

Carlos. Carlos was an undergraduate student who was part of the outreach program with a scholarship. He moved from the Dominican Republic as a young child to the United States and continued to regularly visit family still living in the Dominican Republic. In one of his reflections, he discussed how he struggled in eighth grade with his gay sexuality and that this impacted his identity. He revealed in a class discussion and written reflection that his struggle with sexuality led to depression. He was able to invert that depression into public outreach and worked with several organizations to speak publicly about his struggles so other young people may not have to suffer as much as he did. While in Mexico, he said he felt at home and was very comfortable with himself and his identity.

Ricardo. While Ricardo's family was from Colombia, he felt a strong connection to the people and heritage in Mexico and called himself Latino. He was an undergraduate student participating in the scholarship outreach program. During class discussions, Ricardo listened intently and connected with the other participants, though with few personal comments. However, his written reflections were very thoughtful, as he articulated many of his emotions during the study abroad experience. Ricardo was an excellent supporter of all students during the program with his gentle demeanor and eagerness to listen.

Jimena. Jimena was an undergraduate student who was part of the outreach program with a scholarship. Being a part of this study abroad program was particularly poignant for Jimena. While in Mexico, she was able to reunite with family from the interior of Mexico she had not seen since she was three. Jimena had feelings of guilt and then pain over the fact that she could physically be with her father's family while he could not reconnect with his own mother across the border due to his immigration status. She self-identified as Mexican, Mexican-American, and Latina.

Celia. Celia was an undergraduate student participating in the scholarship outreach program focusing on a degree in business administration. Prior to high school, she migrated from Colombia to the United States by her own choice for her education. This was an unusual circumstance of immigrant youth, and we suspect the agency she was able to employ in that decision carried forward into an agentic approach to her undergraduate studies, as well. While in the United States, she gravitated toward people who spoke Spanish and shared similar adjacent cultures and heritages. Celia was warm, outgoing, and outspoken in ways that helped co-construct knowledge during the trip.

Oscar. At 19, Oscar was the youngest undergraduate participant who was part of the outreach program with scholarship. He identified his family heritage to be from Puerto Rico and Spain and talked a lot during class about his grandfather who was an artist from Puerto Rico. The U.S. colonization of Puerto Rico was expressed in his writing as a point of connection he felt regarding the perils of coloniality. While in Mexico, he felt a greater connection to his Boricua (his preferred term for Puerto Rican) heritage and identity. Throughout the program, Oscar provided facts and information about the history, native plants, and geographic sites in Mexico. His favorite animal was the axolotl, and the entire group enjoyed learning about its uniqueness as a species native to Mexico.

In this program, we created a space where we were our whole selves with our own voices, experiences, culture, and languages coming together to form relationships and a unique bond. Traveling to Mexico with these Latinx students felt different than going with a group of White students or a majority of White students.

A Note on the Racial Positionality of the Authors and Program Directors

We are a distinct group of authors, and we show facets of who we are to encourage the reader to consider engaging in similar kinds of work. We also argue that while we advocate for creating spaces that center Latinx individuals, those creating the spaces do not have to be Latinx. The eldest of us has had a PhD the least amount of time and was technically a student on this experience, though Marks participated as a co-researcher and co-author with Kasun. Marks is a White, Jewish woman with a working-class background from the urban South who had already been full-time faculty at a nearby university in the Atlanta area for over 15 years.

Kasun is also White and working class from West Virginia and was in her third year as faculty at the Atlanta area university from which we ran the program. We mention these class positionings and religious minority positioning as entry points to understanding being positioned as 'other'. Jefferies is a native of Argentina and a first-generation immigrant to the United States. He has been running heritage study programs in Latin America for 15 years, while also engaging in transnational research in Mexico and Puerto Rico. All are former public school teachers from throughout the United States.

References

Adkins, R. & Messerly, B. (2019). Toward decolonizing education abroad: Moving beyond the self/other dichotomy. In E. Brewer & A. Ogden (Eds.), *Critical perspectives on integrating education abroad into undergraduate education*. Stylus Publishing, LLC, Sterling, VA.

Anzaldúa, G. (1987). How to tame a wild tongue. *Borderlands: The new mestiza- la frontera* (pp. 75–86). San Francisco: Aunt Lute Book Company.

Battiste, M. (2000). *Reclaiming Indigenous voice and vision*. Vancouver: UBC Press.

Battiste, M. (2013). *Decolonizing education: Nourishing the learning spirit*. Vancouver, BC: Purich Publishing.

Belenky, M., Clinchy, B., Goldberger, N., & Tarule, J. (1986). *Women's ways of knowing: The development of self, voice, and mind* (2nd ed.). New York, NY: Basic Books.

Blackwell, K. (2018). Why people of color need spaces without white people. *The Arrow*, open access.

Blake, D., Gasman, M., Esmieu, P., Castro Samayoa, A., & Cener, J. (2020). Culturally relevant study abroad for students of color: Lessons from the Frederick Douglass global fellowship in London. *Journal of Diversity in Higher Education*, *13*(2), 158–168. https://doi.org/10.1037/dhe0000112

Burgo, C. (2020). The impact of study abroad on Spanish heritage language learners. *Journal of Latinos and Education*, *19*(3), 304–312. https://doi.org/10.1080/15348431.2018.1518139

Chang, A. (2017). "Call me a little critical if you will": Counterstories of Latinas studying abroad in Guatemala. *Journal of Hispanic Higher Education*, *16*(1), 3–23.

Cortina, R., Alcoff, L. M., Green Stocel, A., & Esteva, G. (2019). Decolonial trends in higher education: Voices from Latin America. *Compare: A Journal of Comparative and International Education*, *49*(3), 489–506.

Doerr, N. (2015). Learner subjects in study abroad: Discourse of immersion, hierarchy of experience and their subversion through situated learning. *Discourse: Studies in the Cultural Politics of Education*, *36*(3), 369–382.

Esteva, G. (2018). Figueroa "Más allá de la tormenta", Revista CoPaLa. Año 3, número 6, julio-diciembre 2018. pp. 7–27. ISSN: 2500-8870. Disponible en: http://www.revistacopala.co

Four Arrows (2016). *Point of Departure: Returning to our more authentic worldview for education and survival*. Charlotte, NC: Information Age Publishing, Inc.

Grande, S. (2015). *Red pedagogy: Native American social and political thought* (10th ed.). Lanham, Maryland: Rowman & Littlefield.

Guerrero, E., Jr. (2006). *The road less traveled: Latino students and the impact of studying abroad.* (Unpublished Doctoral Dissertation). University of California Los Angeles, Retrieved from Dissertation Abstracts International. (AAT 3249418)

Hartman, E., Reynolds, N. P., Ferrarini, C., Messmore, N., Evans, S., Al-Ebrahim, B., & Brown, J. M. (2020). Coloniality-decoloniality and critical global citizenship: Identity, belonging and education abroad. *Frontiers: The Interdisciplinary Journal of Study Abroad, XXXII*(2), 33–59.

Institute of International Education. (2019). *Opendoors: Report on international education exchange 2019.* New York: Institute of International Education. Retrieved from www.iie.org

Kaneria, A. J., Kasun, G. S., & Marks, B. W. (2022). "Why Am I the One Who Gets to Go to Mexico?": Nepantlera Bridging Among Latinx Students in a Decolonial Study Abroad Program. *Teachers College Record, 124*(9), 122–148. https://doi.org/10.1177/01614681221132942

Kasun, G. S. (2017). A decolonizing study abroad program in Mexico for pre-service teachers: Taking on the cultural mismatch between teachers and students. In A. Heejung (Ed.), *Efficacy and implementation of study abroad programs for P-12 teachers* (pp. 190–205). Hershey, PA: IGI Global.

Keating, A. (2013). *Transformation now! toward a post-oppositional politics of change.* Urbana, IL: University of Illinois Press.

Kimmerer, R. (2013). *Braiding sweetgrass: Indigenous wisdom, scientific knowledge, and the teachings of plants.* Canada: Milkweed Editions.

Manitoba Council for International Cooperation. (2020). *Sustainable foundations: A guide for teaching the sustainable development goals* [pdf]. Retrieved from https://sdgs.un.org

Marijuan, S., & Sanz, C. (2018). Expanding boundaries: Current and new directions in study abroad research and practice. *Foreign Language Annals, 51*(1), 185–204.

Marks, B. (2022). *Decolonial connectivity: A study abroad program in Mexico.* (Unpublished Doctoral Dissertation). Georgia State University

Marqués-Pascual, L. (2021). The impact of study abroad on Spanish heritage learners' writing development. In R. Pozzi, T. Quan, & C. Escalante (Eds.), *Heritage Speakers of Spanish and Study Abroad* (pp. 199–216). New York: Routledge.

McLaren, P. (2015). *Life in schools: An introduction to critical pedagogy in the foundations of education.* New York, NY: Routledge.

Mignolo, W. (2011). *The darker side of western modernity: Global futures, decolonial options.* Durham, NC: Duke University Press.

Mitchell, L. (2019). *Storytelling in a culturally responsive classroom: Opening minds, shifting perspectives, and transforming imaginations.* Lanham, MD: Lexington Books.

Mohanty, C. T. (2003). *Feminism without borders: Decolonizing theory, practicing solidarity.* Durham, NC: Duke University Press.

Nguyen, S. (2014). 'F' is for family, friend, and faculty influences: Examining the communicated messages about study abroad at a Hispanic-serving institution (HSI). *International Education, Spring,* 77–93.

Pirbhai-Illich, F., Pete, S., & Martin, F. (2017). *Culturally responsive pedagogy: Working towards decolonization, indigeneity and interculturalism.* Switzerland: Palgrave Macmillan.

Pirbhai-Illich, F., & Martin, F. (2019). Decolonizing teacher education in immersion contexts: Working with space, place, and boundaries. In D. Martin, & E. Smolcic (Eds.), *Redefining teaching competence through immersive programs: Practices for culturally sustaining classrooms* (pp. 65–93). London: Palgrave Macmillan. doi:10.1007/978-3-030-24788-1

Prakash, M., & Esteva, G. (1998). *Escaping education: Living as learning within grass-roots cultures* (Counterpoints; Vol. 36 ed.). New York: Peter Lang.

Quijano, A. (2000). Coloniality of power, ethnocentrism, and Latin America. *Nepantla, 1*(3), 533–580.

Raymondi, M. (2005). *Latino students explore racial and ethnic identity in a global context.* (Unpublished Doctoral Dissertation). State University of New York, Binghamton.

Rubin, K. (2004). Going 'home' to study. *International Educator, 13*(1), 26.

Santos, B. D. S. (2016). *Epistemologies of the south: Justice against epistemicide.* New York, NY: Routledge.

Smith, L. T. (2013). *Decolonizing methodologies: Research and indigenous peoples* (2nd ed.). London: Zed Books Ltd.

Smolcic, E., & Katunich, J. (2017). Review article: Teachers crossing borders: A review of the research into cultural immersion field experience for teachers. *Teaching and Teacher Education, 62*, 47–59. https://doi.org/10.1016/j.tate.2016.11.002

Shively, R. (2016). Heritage language learning in study abroad. In Pascual y D. Cabo (Eds.), *Advances in Spanish as a heritage language* (pp. 259–280). John Benjamins Publishing Company.

Shively, R. (2018). Spanish heritage speakers studying abroad. In K. Potowski (Ed), *The Routledge Handbook of Spanish as a Heritage Language* (pp. 403–419). New York: Routledge.

Tuck, E., McKenzie, M., & McCoy, K. (2014). Land education: Indigenous, post-colonial, and decolonizing perspective on place and environmental education research. *Environmental Education Research, 20*, 1–23.

Tuck, E., & Yang, K. W. (2012). Decolonization is not a metaphor. *Decolonization: Indigeneity, Education & Society, 1*(1), 1–40.

Walsh, C. (2007). Shifting the geopolitics of critical knowledge: Decolonial thought and cultural studies 'others' in the Andes. *Cultural Studies, 21*(2–3), 224–239.

Wick, D., Willis, T., Rivera, J., Lueker, E., & Hernandez, M. (2019). Assets-based learning abroad: First-generation Latinx college students leveraging and increasing community cultural wealth in Costa Rica. *Frontiers: The Interdisciplinary Journal of Study Abroad, 31*(2), 63–85.

Willis, T. (2015). "And still we rise...": Microaggressions and intersectionality in the study abroad experiences of black women. *Frontiers: The Interdisciplinary Journal of Study Abroad, XXVI*, 209–229.

Wynter, S. (2003). Unsettling the coloniality of Being/Power/Truth/Freedom: Towards the human, after man, its overrepresentation--an argument. *CR: The New Centennial Review, 3*(3), 257–337. https://doi.org/10.1353/ncr.2004.0015

Yosso, T. (2005). Whose culture has capital? A critical race theory discussion of community cultural wealth. *Race ethnicity and Education*, *8*(1), 69–91.

Zavala, M. (2016). Design, participation, and social change: What design in grassroots spaces can teach learning scientists. *Cognition & Instruction*, *34*(3), 236–249.

2 Decolonizing Study Abroad
Purposeful Design of the Program and Research Approach

This chapter describes the creation of spaces for students to engage what should be their birth rights—access to their cultures and heritages. The purposeful design of these programs does not reproduce a 'students as tourists' approach. In order for this to happen, the faculty and coordinators need a degree of flexibility in how they recruit students, plan activities, choose locations, create partnerships, decide where students will room and eat, find collaborative partners, and so on. Most study abroad programs are guided by a third-party provider who ends up designing and planning most of the out-of-class activities for students, and, with some exceptions, these compare with tourist agencies that reproduce a tourist experience that uncritically and voyeuristically looks at the Other, frames it as a consumer activity, and keeps students in a homogenous comfort zone (Adkins & Messerly, 2019).

The greater U.S. university system, at the same time, prefers faculty to work with third-party providers and privileges this kind of arrangement because of aversion to liability and financial concerns. These are part of the overall pressure to neoliberalize academia. What we mean is that the university system is transitioning from the notion of university as a space for the creation and contemplation of old and new knowledge through intra-and interdisciplinary study to the notion of being a space where workers are *trained*, with the goal of growing the economy. But in order to avoid reproducing neoliberal, colonizing experiences, study abroad should rely on faculty having the liberty to tie class objectives to the kinds of decolonial experiences that students have during the trip.

In this chapter, we delve into effective ways to recruit first-generation Latinx college students, which run counter, at times, to institutional thinking about recruiting. We describe how to make education abroad experiences accessible and meaningful for them, how to choose locations that align with the objectives of the course, and how to work toward a curriculum that honors the students' and community partners' home language. The chapter also highlights the dreams and overviews of programmatic designers wherein the visions are embedded in daily work of the

DOI: 10.4324/9781003320111-3

programming (including predeparture experience). In doing so, the chapter highlights elements of the program that has run for several years out of Cuernavaca, Mexico, toward the benefit of claiming the birthright of Latinx youth.

We foreground barriers particular to students of color in order for the reader to better understand why we go to these lengths of program design. The cost of study abroad prohibits participation from students with a broader range of socioeconomic backgrounds (Wanner, 2009). According to (Quezada, 2004) less than 10% of study abroad students are from the economically disadvantaged. As with other essential programs in higher education, funding should be a commitment that can be implemented through study abroad scholarships making the experience more equitably affordable (Wanner, 2009). Two characteristics of study abroad programs are noted as particular barriers to participation. One program characteristic is described as a lack of programs in places of interest to students of color (Kasravi, 2009; Nguyen, 2014; Sweeney, 2013; Willis, 2015). The other program characteristic that limits students' of color's participation in study abroad is not seeing how the experience advances their career inspirations (Guerrero, 2006; Kasravi, 2009; Picard et al., 2009). We recognize that travel outside national borders also appears an unnecessary luxury to more working-class students who are often helping their entire families meet financial burdens, as well.

At the end of this chapter, we explain the research approach we took to create our questions, collect data, analyze it, and shape it into what is then presented in the following chapters. We examine the qualitative methodological points of view that inform the book: from autoethnography to participant observation and open-ended interviews. We complement this perspective with the opportunity to closely observe and interact with our program participants on a daily basis during the program, using participant observation (Spradley, 1980) and open-ended interviews (Denzin & Lincoln, 1994) to elicit how creating spaces 'outside of Whiteness' (Blackwell, 2018) creates opportunities for reclaiming and healing (Zavala, 2016).

Program Planning

All of us, as authors, have experiences in international programs abroad with predominantly White students, both as undergraduates ourselves and/or as program advisors. For instance, when Kasun was faculty at a predominantly Mormon university in the U.S. Intermountain West, there was little hope she could succeed in taking a mostly Black, Indigenous, and People of Color (BIPOC) group of students when they comprised less than 10% of the entire student population at the time. That said, with her shift in institution to one that graduates the most Black students annually out of all U.S. universities, her possibilities and the imagination of what is possible with her students have dramatically changed. This means embracing a mentality about recruiting and program design that will center BIPOC students while also considering the dynamics of the relationships with the people in the 'host' country. Jefferies, on the other hand, had experiences which became increasingly rich the more Latinx students he took to the point where he worked to make it clear that predominantly Latinx students' experiences would be the focus of the study abroad explicitly. These comparative lenses have been useful in our program design and research approaches.

Figure 2.1 illustrates who went on the program experience we describe in this book and we compare the annual statistics for U.S. study abroad:

The students on this trip were almost entirely Latinx. We believe this was due in large part because of the selected location (Mexico) and how it resonates with the largest Latinx population at the university, predominantly first- and second-generation Mexican-origin students. Similarly, this was my (Kasun) third year taking students from my university, and students said they had heard about the program through word-of-mouth as well as connections with the largest Latinx student support office on campus. At my university, approximately 16% of the students were Latinx at the time of writing.

In order to attract such a high proportion of Latinx students, I made targeted recruiting efforts on a campus that was less than 16% Latinx. My program was open to all students, including students at the undergraduate and graduate levels, but I especially hoped to take Latinx students. Based on prior experiences of taking Latinx youth to Mexico for my program, I knew the students often benefited far more from the program in terms of their own identity and linguistic renewals/restorations.

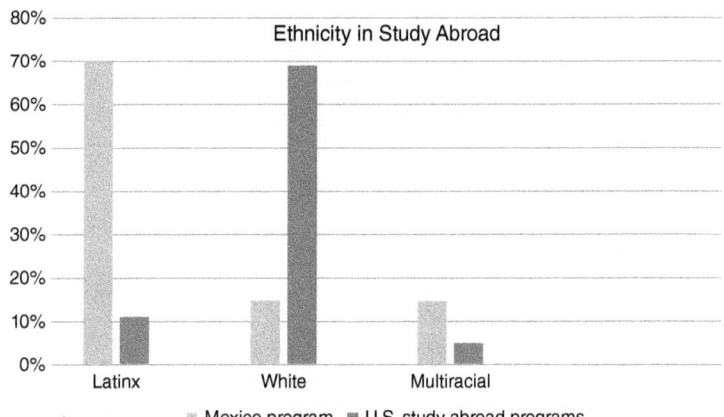

Figure 2.1 Cultural Diversity in the Mexico Study Abroad Program.

One of the highest-yield strategies for recruiting Latinx youth was working directly with the Latinx student outreach organization on campus. I had worked with the campus director on an initiative related to advocacy for immigrant communities, and I approached the director during the recurring meetings to suggest she work to recruit Latinx students. The director seemed persuaded by the impacts of the program and allowed me to guest speak to recruit the students. Perhaps more importantly, the director had access to a since-completed scholarship fund which could be accessed to support participation of a select group of students who were already receiving scholarships. They even negotiated a set number of scholarship students who might attend. This provided six students' funding for this specific program. I met directly on campus with any affiliated youth who were interested and answered many personal emails related to the program. As another example, to additionally target Latinx students, I approached other Latinx recipients of another scholarship to become dual language immersion teachers by guest speaking at some of their on-campus classes. While it was complicated with their preservice teaching placements at time, several Latinx students were very interested. One ultimately entered the program. Another student was strongly encouraged by her own advisor in her counseling master's program that the experience might help bolster her own identity. I met personally with her in her office on campus to explore her perspective on how it might support objecttives.

Language Institute Connections

This program was designed in concert with the director of a language and culture institute, CILAC Freire, Martha Mata. The two-week study abroad program took place in Cuernavaca, Morelos, which is 85 kilometers (1 hour 45 minutes) south of Mexico City. We arrived in Mexico City and stayed one night before driving (by van) to Cuernavaca. For this school and its employees, we are using actual names with their supporting endorsements. Martha is the widow of the founder and former director, Jorge Torres, with whom I (Kasun) had worked for several years in prior programs. The language school, consisting of four cozy classrooms that fit eight people each, had existed for over 30 years. It endured the city of Cuernavaca's ups and downs, from being a hotbed of intellectual and artistic fervent for decades, starting in the 1960s, to becoming a less-desired vacation location due to an increase in drug cartel movement and government corruption. Swine flu and a federal crackdown on some Mexican drug cartels in the mid-2000s had also diminished the entire country's profile as a tourist destination, and over half of Cuernavaca's former language schools closed around that time.

CILAC Freire survived and continues to exist, in large part, due to its commitment to community, including all the families and organizations who have supported its mission of being a space that actively and overtly supports social justice movements throughout the world with a basis in Brazilian theorist Paolo Freire's notions of changing the world through the world and liberatory pedagogy. Teachers usually are affiliated for ten or more years and are invested in their own professional development. For instance, CILAC Freire was the first language school in Mexico to offer an LGBTQIA+-focused language and culture study program in Mexico. More recently, they hosted the first-ever Dreamers programs wherein Mexican-origin and Mexican-born youth who had registered as 'Dreamers' to create a pathway to citizenship returned to their birthland for the first time. The programs received positive international press and were life-changing for many students who would not have otherwise been able to have visited Mexico.

There is a unique background to my (Kasun) work with CILAC Freire that we mention to highlight how important relationships are, as well as meaningful networks based in authentic care. When I was about to start a tenure-track faculty position at Utah State University in 2013, a mentor and faculty member who had recruited me, Martha Whitaker, had already established a deep connection with CILAC Freire.

When I interviewed for the job with Utah State University in 2013, Whitaker encouraged me to take up the relationship toward starting my own study abroad program. In what might be called coincidence, it turned out that my University of Texas doctoral advisor, Luis Urrieta, Jr., had run successful programs with CILAC Freire a few years prior. Due to my trusting relationship with my advisor and the resounding endorsement he gave to the school—especially the couple who ran it at the time, Jorge Torres and Martha Mata—Kasun moved forward with great momentum to build that relationship and program (which I achieved in 2014). Since 2013, I have visited or led programs with CILAC Freire nearly every year, taking my two children with me to continue community building. In 2018, during a Fulbright award I held in the state of Hidalgo, Torres tragically died due to kidney failure. My family went immediately to the funeral as part of our sense of solidarity with the survivors and the school community. I feel my own children belong as much to the CILAC Freire family as to communities in the United States in which I am enmeshed, if not more so.

We recognize that not everyone can have the benefit of these fortuitous relationships, but we note that there are times when being open, intuitive, and authentically relational (as opposed to transactional) creates the conditions wherein this openness allows for the right people to connect to be generative. Jefferies has similarly thick connections with heritage study partners in Mexico and Puerto Rico and attests that these relationships are foundational to the success of a carefully vetted and crafted program

Decolonizing Study Abroad 33

Figure 2.2 Jorge Torres and Martha Mata, former director and current director, respectively, of CILAC Freire. Photo taken by Kasun, author.

for the students' intended decolonial experiences. We also invoke the adage, 'Hablando, se hacen las cosas', that by talking, things get done. Through relationships and networks, indeed, things have gotten done, and we turn now toward relationships with the homestay families.

Homestay Families

During a major economic downturn in the 2010s, the CILAC Freire homestay families pitched in for the maintenance and cleaning of the school by taking turns on who would clean the building, something unheard of in other institutions where homestay families work more strictly on a contractual basis. The same homestay families have participated in workshops to learn about issues such as sexuality, human rights, veganism, and the Zapatista movement, among others. Homestay families have reported their own growth as individuals and as part of the school collective over the decades.

The language school in Cuernavaca coordinated the homestays by determining the host families and selecting the students who stayed at each home. Most of the homestay families were led by older women who often had formative experiences as mothers, working professionals, activists, and care providers. Of the 12 or so affiliated families, most of them have been involved for well over a decade. The majority have connections to and often current beliefs in Catholicism, usually a somewhat or very progressive form of Catholicism. Although, the host families are sensitive to other religions, learning about the diversity of religions through workshops at CILAC-Freire. In an interview with one of the host families, Marks listened as the host mom related the story of removing a cross from the bedroom wall for a student. Nearly all homes had intergenerational family members living with them, and most were considered, by Mexican standards, some level of middle class (usually a lower middle class). This means the visiting students had hot water, three excellent meals a day, and a comfortable individual bed in addition to an attentive host mom who would consistently look out for and genuinely worry about the experience of the students. The lunchtime meal, a mainstay of Mexican cultures, was foundational to the students getting to spend hours with the host families in conversation and learning about Mexico. The host families were attentive to this aspect as well as any student dietary needs and requests.

At the risk of overstating their hospitality, we also recognize these families lived in the Global South and are unduly impacted by an unjust global economic system that creates pressures for the need to support their livelihood through hosting. While these families in large part do this labor for economic gain, after my decade of knowing them and Marks's direct research with them, it is clear they also do this as genuine labor of love. This is represented in some of the interviews with the homestay families; for example, 'I talked to Martha to tell her that I wanted to receive students. Because having people from Airbnb is impersonal. They just have breakfast and we talk a little. I like to convivir with others – to know the people, to know their traditions, to know their life stories and to share mine. This is what happens with students from CILAC Freire'. We have engaged different homestay families with CILAC Freire and attest to the deep sense of care they experienced firsthand. This was manifested as well in visits to other host families and the reports of participating students.

Site

The program was situated in the medium-sized city of Cuernavaca, Mexico, a two-hour bus ride south of Mexico City in the country's interior. It is hilly and has distinct views of nearby mountains which turn green during the rainy season of May through October. The hilliness means streets were often narrow for foot traffic and vehicle traffic. Parts of the city are colonial looking, as if a mirror of the Spanish colonial past, while others are modern with contemporary and exclusive architecture. Many other parts of the city reflect the global problem of limited resources with build-as-you-can housing for the economically poorer. The city is still considered a getaway location for the 20 million-plus inhabitants of Mexico City.

Figure 2.3 One of downtown Cuernavaca's central plazas during public dancing on a Sunday evening. Photo by Marks, author.

Cuernavaca has a long history of being a hotbed of intellectual and artistic creation, though this has waned in the last decade or so due to increased drug cartel activity. Students tour, as one activity, the beautiful Museum Robert Brady, named after its owner, an eccentric artist whose art-filled home was visited by luminaries such as Erich Fromm, Ivan Illich, Josephine Baker, and many others. This is one of the rarer, traditional tourist activities of the program, but it is used for reflection on the contrasts of wealth in Mexico. The city is the capital of the state, Morelos, and has long been considered politically progressive. Activists are well-networked in the city and support current and past social movements, most recently for women's rights, for the disappeared of Mexico, and for the local environment and those nearby who have been custodians of the land for generations. The state is home to Mexican Revolution hero Emiliano Zapata, and his image is found throughout the state in restaurants, galleries, and public buildings.

Each international study participant stayed in a double-occupancy bedroom with a homestay family near the language school. Homestay families provided community resources (transportation, places to meet personal needs) for the study abroad students. We remained in Cuernavaca through the program after an initial stayover in Mexico City for a brief entry into the larger world of, 'What is Mexico?'

Course Curriculum and Activities as Curriculum

International study programs located in the Global South need to acknowledge issues of colonialism through critical reflection and dialogue (Hartman et al., 2020). The Latinx students in this program learned by engaging in meaningful and deliberate class discussions about the complex social realities in Mexico so they could better understand issues such as immigration and transnationalism, issues which are, for them, often very close to the heart and not merely academic (Kasun et al., 2020; Kasun, 2016). In the curriculum of the Spanish language school, the teachers discussed local social issues which were interwoven into the course discussions. These discussions ranged from topics such as class positioning, informal economies, public transportation, connections of communal care and concern for one another, and romantic relationships, among others. These kinds of topics helped students understand better why their own parents might have migrated, how their parents may have fallen in love, what kind of future labor the participants might want to do, perhaps across borders, and how they were more connected with their families in countries of origin. These understandings were built in concert with the formal course material, described below.

Participating in the study abroad program experiences and assignments, the students were part of a three-credit course: *Mexican culture, global movements, and schooling*. Through readings, discussions, and structured curricular experiences, Kasun introduced the cultural, economic, and social issues relating to the language and diversity of Mexican-origin populations specifically. She also centered the students' identities and how they often intersected with the people they planned to meet, including open discussions related to the system of racial oppression, cultural co-identification in enriching ways, and the various kinds of immigration statuses and global economic factors which create immigration flows. Personal stories and testimonials from local activists in the community were powerful ways to connect the study abroad students with the local community. The study abroad program was designed through a decolonial curriculum as a personal and collective journey.

Kasun conceptualized the curriculum through an Indigenous knowledge framework using the *Four Agreements* by Don Miguel Ruiz (1997), an Indigenous author from the Eagle Knight lineage in Mexico. The text is foundational to the work at a non-traditional school the students spent four days at and also an informal code of conduct for the group. The agreements are based on ancient Toltec wisdom and encourage those who embrace them to be reflective, to not take things personally, and to do one's best. Learning about the history and culture of Latinx and Indigenous

Decolonizing Study Abroad 37

people through Indigenous ways of knowing, the Latinx students gained knowledge that was missing from their Western education (Battiste, 2013). The idea was not to replace Western knowledge but to braid Indigenous, Latinx, and other subjugated histories and knowledge together for students to gain an appreciation of the multiplicity of histories and cultures. Other readings ranged from work critical of neoliberalism and its impact on Mexico (e.g. Bigelow, 2006, and related videos) to Kasun's own work on ways of knowing and Mexican-origin transnational populations. The course was decolonial in its orientation from the readings, the way discussions were arranged to be dialogic and inclusive of all voices, and the way community was created from the first of two predeparture curricular sessions.

The course objectives, as noted in the syllabus, were:

1 Students will learn fundamental principles, generalizations, or theories regarding difference, diversity, and ways of knowing and how they relate to movements of immigrants/transnationals and schooling.
2 Students will gain factual knowledge (terminology, classifications, methods, trends) related to Mexican culture, immigration, and schooling in Mexico and the United States.
3 Students will develop specific skills, competencies, and points of view by analyzing and critically evaluating ideas, arguments, and points of view. To do this, students will read and critique texts and articles, participate in class discussions, assignments, and activities, and apply these ideas through practice in Mexico with a non-traditional school.

The kinds of activities selected were pivotal and intentionally crafted, as well.

During the program, we were engaged in 14 intensive days of language and culture studies in Mexico. At the same time, we allowed for flexibility of in-the-moment experiences to support a looping and weaving of understandings. To illustrate, we had planned to visit the Museum of Indomitable Memory (https://museocasadelamemoriaindomita.mx), a memorial to active work to recover Mexico's 100,000+ disappeared individuals from the 1970s, onward. The memorial includes discussions of international connections beyond Mexico's internal political problems to connections with the United States and its support of 'dirty wars' in Latin America, stemming from the 1950s onward. Because we arrived on Mexico's commemoration of Mother's Day, the museum was closed. This opened space for additional spontaneous visits in the heart of Mexico City's historic downtown. While walking the historic Zócalo, or main town square, we observed the usual faith healers performing dances and rituals. Aware that some of these rituals could be more for tourist consumption than real healing, we trusted Martha Mata's and Kasun's instincts to engage one of the healers to put us all into a circle and perform a ritual of connection and healing.

The ritual took over an hour, and he prayed over each one of us while also having us stand in a circle. Such acts in the United States seem generally anathema to usual curricular experiences, but it felt entirely reasonable for those who wanted to participate to do so (two students chose not to). He spoke with each one of us privately for about a minute, and we each agreed he had somehow peered into our deeper recesses of our conscious and unconscious lives. Such observations included letting us know things from who might discover their life's work soon to who would be overcoming a massive fear of commitment. This experience impacted the Latinx students as they reflected upon it in their writings. Ana wrote, 'I had to stand there for what felt like hours as he poured out paragraphs to the other students. When he got to me, his words really resonated with me and they replayed over and over in my head and they still do'. Celia also reflected on the experience, 'I had the opportunity to cleanse my body and mind with two rituals. At the beginning I was a little skeptical, but I realized that they worked and helped me pay better attention to myself'.

Figure 2.4 Ritual healing temazcal/sweat lodge in Cuernavaca. Photo by Marks, author.

Through two-hour course discussions, held at Kasun's short-term apartment and even at the school's pool, as well as at the school in classroom spaces, we reflected at length on our curricular and personal journeys. These were built on students' two-page reflections weaving course readings into purposeful questions that aligned with the experiences of the program. For instance, students had the opportunity to reflect on how they saw the Four Agreements in practice at Caminando Unidos (the organization's real name, used with permission), an informal educational space that provides learning for marginalized youth in Cuernavaca. CILAC Freire also offered a range of talks by local experts which we wove into our reflections. These included, for instance, a local activist who described the Zapatista autonomous Indigenous movement's past two decades of work in both the state of Chiapas and international connections and inspiration as well as a Guatemalan immigrant's stories of work as a Mayan healer and her activist work as a Central American immigrant in Mexico, a perspective often less considered when we discuss migration issues within the United States.

The comradery and solidarity the director and students felt as a group and community happened through a relational environment established in the study abroad program and influenced by the lens of Indigenous ways of knowing. Relationships must be central to the pedagogical approaches in study abroad programs (Pirbhai Illich & Martin, 2019).

Research Methodology

Considering the complex experiences and power dynamics inherent among the students and place of study, we chose a methodology that challenges injustice and social power structures by engaging and interpreting social interactions in a particular setting (Madison, 2020). Madison (2020) contends that 'critical ethnography is always a meeting of multiple sides in an encounter with and among others, one in which there is negotiation and dialogue toward substantial and viable meanings that make a difference in others' worlds' (p. 9). The critical ethnographer identifies and brings forth the stories and experiences of underrepresented people.

Critical Ethnographic Case Study

A case study is different from other methodological approaches as a case study is an analysis and description of 'a single unit or system bounded by space and time' (Hancock & Algozzine, 2017; Yin, 2014). This study was an in-depth exploration from interviews, class discussions, and written reflections (multiple perspectives) in the real-life context of the local community of the study abroad program (Yin, 2014). The group of study abroad students in the program was the unit of analysis for the case study.

As we analyzed the data, we found the group of nine Latinx students were a relevant case study. A case study of a study abroad program is bounded in temporal dimensions such as the two weeks in the study abroad program and spatial dimensions such as the local community of Cuernavaca, Mexico, where the students lived and studied (Yin, 2014). The findings from the research were from various sources of data within the program and grounded in the theoretical framework of relational approaches through a decolonizing lens (Crotty, 1998).

The case study methodology does not describe itself as critical in its approach or analysis of process and data. Therefore, using critical ethnography with case study, we applied a critical approach to focus the design of the program with students of color from the Global North traveling to the Global South as examined through social power structures.

Ethnography is a form of qualitative research from the field of anthropology where the researcher uses the methods of fieldwork and interviews to study a group of people and their culture, which includes shared behaviors and language in a natural setting over a long period of time (Wolcott, 2008). An example of ethnography is the written records by Spanish conquistadores when they encountered the Indigenous people in Mexico. This colonial writing included rich description of Indigenous culture to understand the people they were colonizing (Gonzalez, 2003). A critical ethnography acknowledges power structures and challenges the gaze of inquiry. In a critical ethnography, the written accounts of Indigenous people by the Spanish colonizers would focus on social power structures and a need for agency to create a more equitable system (Gonzalez, 2003; Madison, 2020). Grbich (2013) explains the primary purpose of critical ethnography is to understand how the historical, 'political, economic and social aspects of the culture must be gained through interpretation using critical theory' (p. 56). The criteria for a critical ethnography include issues of power and oppression, social transformation for the participants through a form of action, and identity of the researcher described through reflexivity (Madison, 2020). Researchers using critical ethnography are not the neutral observer as in classical ethnography, but they place themselves in an active position to critique throughout the project. The majority of research using critical ethnography is in situations where there is socioeconomic inequality such as locations in the Global South.

As we examined the data, we critically explored the historical, political, economic, and social culture of the Latinx students in the study abroad program and the communities of the local people. The data and analysis were used to examine social transformation through feelings of solidarity with authentic relationships among the group of study abroad students and reciprocity with the host community. A critical ethnography actively pursues the disruption of the power dynamics between the Global North and the Global South (Madison, 2020). As researchers, we are aware of cultural, sociopolitical, and natural conditions of the domestic spaces within the homestay and the interactions of the study abroad students. We designed this research study to explore the answers to the research question.

How do Latinx students in a short-term study abroad program experience relationship building through a decolonizing lens?

Research Design

This study occurred during a short-term, two-week study abroad program in May 2019. The study abroad program included undergraduate and graduate students traveling from the United States to Mexico. Using a critical ethnographic case study, we examined the existing power structures and personal stories that surround a study abroad program traveling from the Global North to the Global South with Latinx participants.

Data Collection and Instruments

The data we used for this study were from multiple data sources. Data from the participants and homestay families were included to seek diversity of perspectives and a holistic view of relational approaches through decolonization in the context of the study abroad program. The data sources included the following: participant observation, interviews of homestay families, audio recordings of class discussions, student assignments, and written reflections based on photos taken by the participants in the program.

Participant Observation

As participant observers (Spradley, 1980), we engaged in multiple roles with the other students and within the study. First, I (Marks, 2022) was a student taking an academic course, which included participating in all activities of the program. As a student and participant observer, I considered my own rapport and shared experiences with the other participants in the program. My interactions and relationships were interpreted through my own vision, and I saw myself as an older mentor and person with more life experiences than the other participants, including the program coordinator, Kasun. Kasun was a participant observer accustomed to similar experiences but always open to learning from and with her students. Behar (1996) describes a researcher's role using participant observation as a 'vulnerable observer' where the researcher includes their point of view and emotions about a subject or issue in the data and analysis. These reflections on self are only included if they are 'essential to the argument'. Our roles as participant observers meant that we included our own journals with thoughts and feelings about our experiences and relationships with other participants. As researchers, we were interested in the story of the Latinx students and the homestay families. Paying attention to details and starting informal interviews provided information about the context (DeWalt & DeWalt, 2002). Unexpected findings can be very informative and lead an observer in other directions which means we had to be reflexive and make changes to our approach during the program.

Interviews

A focus of ethnographic interviewing is 'to explore the meanings that people ascribe to actions and events in their cultural words, expressed in their own language' (Roulston, 2011, p. 19). The semi-structured questions in the interview guide allowed participants to describe cultural aspects of space, people, activities, and time. I (Marks) interviewed each host family once using open-ended questions and probes that led to personal stories and rich descriptions. This approach was conversational in nature and initiated a nonjudgmental exchange between the homestay families and me. Rubin and Rubin (1995) use the term 'conversational partners' to describe a conversational interview that is reciprocal in nature. The design of each of the questions was meant to elicit answers that evoke feelings about the host families' experience with students and their connections with the language school.

For the research, I conducted interviews with a decolonizing approach by including input from community members and considering my own subjectivities in relation to the participants in the research and the creation of the questions. Each person that was interviewed was a person with history and agency. The interviews I conducted with the assistance of an interpreter/translator were in their native language of Spanish, so they were able to fully express their ideas. My approach to the data was tempered with respect for the homestay families and the local community.

Class Discussions

The six class sessions were audio-recorded and transcribed. The recordings ranged in time from 80 to 120 minutes in length. The audio recordings documented the interactions of the participants and allowed us to hear the dialogue during the class discussions and the emotions expressed by the participants. All participants were present during the six class sessions. I (Kasun) guided the participants in discussions focused on specific themes. We numbered each class session chronologically and identified the class session themes as the following: class session 1—Four agreements;

class session 2—compassion and identity; class session 3—funds of knowledge; class session 4—border; class session 5—Indigenous education; class session 6—connections.

Student Assignments during and after the Program and Document Analysis

The assignments for the course were based on theories regarding difference, diversity, and ways of knowing to critically evaluate ideas, arguments, and points of view related to Mexican culture and immigration. We analyzed the following assignments from the course: critical inquiry reading charts, service learning/field experience written reflections, and participant journals (written reflections to a prompt). Another assignment for this study abroad program was a digital identity photoethnography. In the photoethnography assignment, participants took photos to create a visual representation of their intercultural experience related to history, identity, and culture in Mexico. Then, the participants were instructed to write reflections about each photo by describing what the image represented and meant to them. We examined the written reflections and the way the participants conveyed feelings, values, beliefs, and worldviews within the context of the study abroad program.

Document analysis was the method we used to evaluate the course assignments and the ways connectivity was enacted through the lived experiences and emotions of the participants in the study abroad program. In document analysis, the researcher explores many types of textual information including written documents. According to Boreus and Bergstrom (2017), researchers applying document analysis evaluate the way a topic is portrayed and whether the topic is valued positively or negatively in a specific context. Our analyses evaluated the emotions and beliefs of the Latinx students as they navigated power relations in society and expressed their feelings in the documents. There are different document analysis approaches, and choosing one links a specific methodology to produce an understanding of the text (Boreus & Bergstrom, 2017).

The type of document analysis we used was based on the connections between the concepts of decolonization and the indicated relationships within the context of the written material. Thinking about the protocol, we determined what is decolonizing language and what illustrates relationship building. In order to establish a protocol to apply to all the documents, we linked the theories of decolonization with statements in the documents. The context of the history and politics of the host country of Mexico was acknowledged in the data, which was relevant to the context of the written statements in the course assignments. Our aim was to avoid colonial discourse by refraining from language and discourse that reproduced and privileged Western views while privileging language that was meaningful to the

Latinx students. Through a critical theoretical perspective, we wanted to understand the experiences of the Latinx students in a Global South community using text material to explain the dominant themes that emerged.

Data Analysis

The process to make sense from the transcriptions, text, and reflections involved data analysis (Creswell & Creswell, 2018). Analyzing the data, we examined the links between the political, social, economic, and global structures of inequity between the Global South and the Global North. As critical ethnographers, our 'critical assessment of the diversities and complexities of the location(s) and workings of power relations…should result in recommended strategies for, or personal/participant action toward, empowerment and social justice' (Grbich, 2013, p. 61). The lens of decolonization provided a framework for us to analyze the data and account for unjust systems, relational approaches, and collective work that required action and empowerment.

For this study, we inductively coded the data by being open-minded to all possibilities and creating original codes as we reviewed the data (Saldaña, 2021). According to Smagorinsky (2001), the way texts are juxtaposed allows possibilities 'for connection and continuity across readings through a relationship of codes and concepts' (p. 138). This means we grouped the data into relevant parts and meaningful groupings to determine themes and categories through multiple ways of looking at the texts. The processes of grouping we determined were beneficial for the analysis were the block and file approach and the segmentation approach. In block and file, we captured large chunks of dialogue and statements by participants (Grbich, 2013). We believed this was the best way to present multiple voices and different perspectives in the data with thick, rich descriptions (Geertz, 1973). The disadvantage of block and file was the statements by the participants that created large chunks of data and then grouping the statements. Through segmentation, we divided words and phrases into themes. We found that we gained specific ideas from segmentation but the data became decontextualized, and we needed to create analytic memos to provide context.

From the rich stories and written reflections revealed by the participants, we deciphered and coded the data. For our first cycle of coding, we used In Vivo to code the data. In Vivo refers to the words and phrases of the participants in the data. We thought seeing and using the voice of the participants would be the best way to construct themes and categories based on the data (Madison, 2020; Saldaña, 2021). During a second cycle of coding, we recoded the data using emotion codes and value codes because the participant's emotional reactions and personal experiences were interwoven with beliefs and attitudes. Saldaña (2021) explains that emotion coding applications are for 'deep insight into the participants' perspectives, worldviews, and life conditions' (p. 160), while analysis through values coding explores 'the participant's personal and unique experiences and self-constructed identities from social interaction' (p. 172). The two major themes that emerged were solidarity and community.

Trustworthiness

Discussion of trustworthiness includes the terms 'validity' and 'reliability' to ensure accuracy and credibility within the findings of the study (Creswell & Creswell, 2018; Crotty, 1998). A qualitative study with validity (trustworthiness) achieves accuracy, credibility, and neutrality (Creswell & Creswell, 2018). According to Gonzalez (2003), these terms are colonizing and relate to another term: 'accountability'. Patel (2016) describes accountability as 'synonymous with draconian top-down strategies that seek to measure in order to sanction and surveille' (p. 73). The lens of coloniality looks at accountability as an idea where we need to follow the rules to make sure there is accuracy and validity or my conclusions will not be valid. Beyond accountability, we used the data to tell the story and describe how we made our decisions and conclusions. Although we presented the data accurately, as critical ethnographers, we did not approach the data in a neutral way. We are empathetic to the homestay families and the Latinx students who live within oppressive structures in their daily lives. Using rich, thick description in the findings, we provided a realistic view for the reader. We used quotes from the participants to accurately report their views and to support the story told. Through member checking, we had participants in the study read the final report for accuracy of representation. Including personal notes and descriptions of thoughts was a way for us to be transparent and provide context for the data being presented.

Truthfulness was our aim throughout the process of the study. Our willingness to relate what is in our heads and hearts is also a vulnerable position we put ourselves in this study. Using a decolonizing lens toward the research, we examined our positionality and represented the context authentically. Patel (2016) suggests that research should not be subjugated to a colonizer perspective where knowledge is considered property and universal, but research needs to shift to consider knowledge as 'an entity, specific, mutable, and impermanent itself' (p. 79). Research needs answerability and the need for me to be responsible for my research agenda and not perpetuating coloniality.

Ethics

The focus of qualitative studies is on people and collecting data on the participants (Creswell & Creswell, 2018). In Tisdale's (2004) chapter on ethics in research, she defines two rules for the ethical principle of beneficence: '1) Do no harm and 2) maximize possible benefits and minimize possible harms' (p. 21). The exploration of Latinx students in a study abroad program is more beneficial than harmful to the participants. During the study, we considered rapport to build trust with the participants and commitment to the integrity of the research design. In the course of the orientation that initiated the study abroad program, we made clear the intent of conducting research with the participants. In all data reported, we have protected the identities of the participants. Throughout the study, we intentionally respected all cultural norms (as best we could) in the host community as we explored the experiences of the international study students within the context of the Global South (Mexico). All voices and views in the study are valid and no one view is privileged over others. We actively employed research ethics during the research process, data storage, and reporting of the findings. We hope the study and findings are emancipatory for the participants.

Looking Forward: Quality of International Study Experiences

Our findings ultimately point to how international program faculty need to deepen the decolonial and relational aspects of the program to draw attention to the quality of the experiences of marginalized students. Experiences in study abroad that liberate marginalized students from invalidating past experiences allow consciousness-raising. Study abroad faculty have the responsibility to foster the strengths of underrepresented students in international immersion programs and unleash their feelings to be free to be themselves and validate their experiences and beliefs.

References

Adkins, R. & Messerly, B. (2019). Toward decolonizing education abroad: Moving beyond the self/other dichotomy. In E. Brewer & A. Ogden (Eds.), *Critical perspectives on integrating education abroad into undergraduate education*. Stylus Publishing, LLC, Sterling, VA.

Battiste, M. (2013). *Decolonizing education: Nourishing the learning spirit*. Vancouver, BC: Purich Publishing.

Behar, R. (1996). *The vulnerable observer: Anthropology that breaks your heart*. Boston, MA: Beacon Press.

Bigelow, B. (2006). NAFTA and the roots of migration. In Bill Bigelow (Ed.), *The line between us: Teaching about the border and Mexican immigration*. (pp. 19–27). Milwaukee, WI: Rethinking Schools, Ltd.

Blackwell, K. (2018). Why people of color need spaces without white people. *The Arrow*, open access.

Boreus, K., & Bergstrom, G. (2017). *Analyzing text and discourse*. Los Angeles: Sage.

Creswell, J. W., & Creswell, J. D. (2018). *Research design: Qualitative, quantitative, and mixed methods approaches* (5th ed.). Thousand Oaks, CA: Sage.

Crotty, M. (1998). *The foundations of social research: Meaning and perspective in the research process.* London: Sage.

Denzin, N. K., & Lincoln, Y. S. (1994). *Handbook of qualitative research.* Thousand Oaks, CA: Sage.

DeWalt, K., & DeWalt, B. (2002). *Participant observation: A guide for fieldworkers.* New York: AltaMira.

Geertz, C. (1973). *The interpretation of cultures: Selected essays.* New York: Basic Books.

Gonzalez, M. (2003). An ethics for postcolonial ethnography. In R. Claire (Ed.), *Expressions of ethnography: Novel approaches to qualitative methods* (pp. 77–86). Albany, NY: SUNY Press.

Grbich, C. (2013). *Qualitative data analysis: An introduction* (2nd ed.). Thousand Oaks, CA: Sage.

Guerrero, E., Jr. (2006). *The road less traveled: Latino students and the impact of studying abroad.* (Unpublished Doctoral Dissertation). University of California Los Angeles, Retrieved from Dissertation Abstracts International. (AAT 3249418)

Hancock, D. & Algozzine, B. (2017). *Doing case study research: A practical guide for beginning researchers* (3rd ed.). New York: Teachers College Press.

Hartman, E., Reynolds, N. P., Ferrarini, C., Messmore, N., Evans, S., Al-Ebrahim, B., & Brown, J. M. (2020). Coloniality-decoloniality and critical global citizenship: Identity, belonging and education abroad. *Frontiers: The Interdisciplinary Journal of Study Abroad, XXXII*(2), 33–59.

Kasravi, J. (2009). *Factors influencing the decision to study abroad for students of color: Moving beyond the barriers.* (Unpublished Doctoral dissertation). University of Minnesota, (AAT 3371866)

Kasun, G.S., Hernández, T., & Montiel, H. (2020). The engagement of transnationals in Mexican university classrooms: Points of entry towards recognition among future English teachers. *Multicultural Perspectives, 22*(1), 37–45. https://doi.org/10.1080/15210960.2020.1728273

Kasun, G. S. (2016). Interplay of a way of a knowing among Mexican-origin transnationals: Chaining to the border and to transnational communities. *Teachers College Record 119*(9), 1–32.

Madison, D. S. (2020). *Critical ethnography: Method, ethics, and performance* (3rd ed.). SAGE Publications Inc. https://doi.org/10.4135/9781452233826

Marks, B. (2022). *Decolonial connectivity: A study abroad program in Mexico.* (Unpublished Doctoral Dissertation). Georgia State University.

Nguyen, S. (2014). 'F' is for family, friend, and faculty influences: Examining the communicated messages about study abroad at a Hispanic-serving institution (HSI). *International Education, Spring,* 77–93.

Patel, L. (2016). *Decolonizing educational research: From ownership to answerability* (Series in critical narratives ed.). New York: Routledge.

Picard, E., Bernardino, F., & Ehigiator, K. (2009). Global citizenship for all: Low minority students participation in study abroad-seeking strategies for success. In R. Lewin (Ed.), *The handbook of practice and research in study abroad* (pp. 321–345). New York, NY: Routledge.

Pirbhai Illich, F., & Martin, F. (2019). Decolonizing teacher education in immersion contexts: Working with space, place, and boundaries. In D. Martin & E. Smolcic (Eds.), *Redefining teaching competence through immersive programs: Practices for culturally sustaining classrooms* (pp. 65–93). London: Palgrave Macmillan. https://doi.org/10.1007/978-3-030-24788-1

Quezada, R. (2004). Beyond educational tourism: Lessons learned while student teaching abroad. *International Education Journal, 5*(4), 458–465.

Roulston, K. (2011). *Reflective interviewing: A guide to theory and practice.* Thousand Oaks: SAGE.

Rubin, H. & Rubin, I. (1995). *Qualitative interviewing: The art of hearing data.* Thousand Oaks: SAGE.

Ruiz, D. M. (1997). *The four agreements: A Toltec wisdom book.* San Rafael, CA: Amber-Allen.

Saldaña, J. (2021). *The coding manual for qualitative researchers.* Los Angeles, CA: Sage.

Smagorinsky, P. (2001). If meaning is constructed, what is it made from? Toward a cultural theory of reading. *Review of Educational Research, 71*(1), 133–169.

Spradley, J. (1980). *Participant observation.* New York: Holt, Rinehart, and Winston.

Sweeney, K. (2013). Inclusive excellence and underrepresentation of students of color in study abroad. *Frontiers: The Interdisciplinary Journal of Study Abroad, XXIII*, 1–21.

Tisdale, K. (2004). Being vulnerable and being ethical within research. In K. de Marrais, & S. Lapan (Eds.), *Foundations for research: Methods of inquiry in education and social sciences* (pp. 13–30) Lawrence Erlbaum Associates.

Wanner, D. (2009). Study abroad and language: From maximal to realistic models. In R. Lewin (Ed.). *The handbook of practice and research in study abroad* (pp. 346–364). New York, NY: Routledge.

Willis, T. (2015). "And still we rise…": Microaggressions and intersectionality in the study abroad experiences of black women. *Frontiers: The Interdisciplinary Journal of Study Abroad, XXVI*, 209–229.

Wolcott, H. (2008). *Ethnography: A way of seeing* (2nd ed.). Walnut Creek, CA: Sage.

Yin, R. (2014). *Case study research: Design and methods* (5th ed.). California: Sage.

Zavala, M. (2016). Design, participation, and social change: What design in grassroots spaces can teach learning scientists. *Cognition & Instruction 34*(3), 236–249.

3 Pedagogical Strategies to Delve Within

A Decolonial Turn toward Renewed Community

In the windowless public university classroom, 12 students and I (Kasun) began to get to know each other predeparture. Each student had been given markers and a sheet of plain white paper to make a name tent so the others could all see each of the participants' names. I had explained parts of her background, being a first-generation college student, bilingual, beginning to learn Spanish at age 17, and raising her two kids bilingually and multiculturally. I shared:

> Study abroad completely changed who I am, thanks to my scholarship transferring to my studies in Mexico for two semesters. It allowed me to reconsider my own father's death, because I shifted from White culture which makes it hard to talk about people who have passed on to a culture which allows space for the Day of the Dead, for instance. I remember how the homestay family who hosted me in Mexico talked about the dad in their family who had died. They would laugh and even be in tears as they remembered him frequently, despite his having died ten years prior. I remember thinking, 'Oh, this is possible to talk about and still love someone who has died!' That was the beginning of learning how different life is in Mexico, and how much we can learn from each other in these exchanges, especially when it comes from learning with those who still hold subjugated knowledges.

I said I wanted them all to take full advantage of what Mexico could teach them, and that the program was structured for them to stop and ask questions and reflect deeply on their learning. I reiterated that the intention was that the students would develop a community and that the first step was really knowing each other, beginning with their names. The students then shared their name preferences as she called roll. I worked to use Spanish pronunciation, rolling rs when it was merited, asking students which version(s) of their names they preferred. I was explicit that names are the foundation of how we relate to each other and that students deserve to have their names pronounced correctly, not butchered into

Anglicized versions such as teachers shifting names from 'Juan' to 'John' for the 'sake of convenience'. Several students spontaneously shared their own scars related to such school-sanctioned events of misusing their names in their U.S. public education experiences. When I tried to call the first name of Ana, which was *Agustina*, Ana told her she usually goes by Ana. I then asked, 'Well, which do you prefer?'

Ana explained, 'Well, my mom took a Spanish name, took the last vowel off to make it sound like English, and it has this funny spelling. Honestly no one here can say my first name right, and it would be nice to go by that. So, yeah, let's go by *Agustina*!' And she remained that for the entire trip and still into her continued relationship with program participants. This was one of the early ways I, along with the participation of the students, co-constructed a decolonial approach and foundation of the program, by starting with students' agency and considerations of their names.

***

In this chapter, we describe the decolonial pedagogical activities that we planned and engaged in the context of study within, reflections and observations about their implementation, and the impact that these activities have for our students. One example of a decolonial pedagogical strategy is reciprocal relationship building. We engage the term 'reciprocity' as a decolonial way to construct relationships and thinking around them (Cajete, 2000; Four Arrows, 2016). When people are engaged reciprocally, it is around an ethos of balance and harmony, not score-keeping, for instance. These kinds of relationships mirror the ways Mother Earth maintains balance (Kimmerer, 2013), and these points are discussed with students prior to departure. The learning that occurred in both structured and spontaneous experiences during the study abroad program was impactful, in large part, due to the relational component. Throughout the program, the students were unlearning the influence of the dominant culture and collectively learning compassion and collaboration.

During the international study program, students were vulnerable and interacted within a safe community by recognizing the humanity within each other and connecting in meaningful ways. They shared individual stories from a socially situated personal history and foreground their struggles as minoritized people in a White-dominant society. The trust and understanding developed in the program were the basis for developing relationships within the group. For instance, one student stated, 'I wanted to know them forever, but I guess that's what happens when you feel safe'. This was typical of the sense of closeness in relationships formed during the experience.

Pedagogical Strategies to Delve Within 51

This chapter provides observation and interview data on how different pedagogical events 'outside of Whiteness' helped students reclaim and rename their identities—particularly in carefully scaffolded conversations—not by exploring the 'Other' in a foreign land but by getting to know themselves 'within' in a deeper way. In the study abroad program, the Latinx students challenged their missing and erased heritage in spaces in the United States.

Context of Pedagogies Employed

The Latinx students in the study abroad program noted how lived experiences in the United States lack outwardly expressed emotions with others and a lack of connection because people in the dominant culture in the United States often do not reveal their true selves and do not speak from the heart. By connecting with each other, the students disrupted feelings of isolation by openly sharing lived experiences of feeling marginalized by the dominant culture in the United States. Being in Mexico brought forth physical feelings of being a part of somewhere without judgment. Connections between the students created a space where they were able to be their fuller selves with their own voices, experiences, culture, and languages while forming a community.

The Latinx students' interaction in planned experiences and spontaneous activities within the study abroad program triggered complicated feelings about themselves and family. Throughout the program, the Latinx students connected to themselves and the local community while acknowledging the impact of colonization on historical, political, and economic systems in the Global South. These complex realities of colonizing 'within' and 'without' impacted the lives of the Latinx students through the understanding of unequal systems of socioeconomics, language, and education (Saavedra & Nymark, 2008). The students had an awareness and openly discussed how they arrived in Mexico with an additional privilege (U.S. citizenship as well as material resources) that many Mexicans inside Mexico did not have while also recognizing imbalances elsewhere, such as the use of Spanish in the United States when their ancestors had spoken Indigenous heritage languages that were often wiped out by Spanish.

These systems shaped the Latinx student lives through marginalization and oppression within the United States. The Latinx students' recognition of struggle was a commonality that provided a basis for relationships between themselves and the local community. Along with common interests, the Latinx students acknowledged and respected the differences among themselves and the people of Mexico. Saavedra and Nymark (2008) describe Anzaldua's 'New Tribalism' as an inclusive feminism that is 'about how we/you/they can witness how we are in each other' (p. 268), akin to the reciprocity of relationship building mentioned above. Connections made through the 'New Tribalism' are ways we 'form alliances with those who are also feeling and living the historical and contemporary effects of Western hegemonic policies, juridical discourses, and economic disenfranchisement' (p. 268). Indeed, the experience of the program was, in many ways, a series of connections toward new tribalisms that transcend the older, more proscribed understandings of tribalism toward Anzaldúa's 'mundo zurdo' (left-handed world) (Anzaldúa, 1981), a world where many worlds fit among this new tribalism. Following is a close-up example of how we started crafting that new set of alliances early on.

During the first weekend, all but one of the Latinx students (one student visited her extended family, meeting them for the first time) participated in a temazcal ritual, a ceremony based on pre-Colombian/Indigenous principles. This was an extra activity and not part of the formal program. We were there because we were open to experiencing something new and not because it was 'mandatory'. This Indigenous ritual was symbolic to entering the womb to heal the spirit, body, and mind. In Mesoamerica, the temazcal is often in the shape of a half sphere, with one entrance that must be crawled through and where participants eventually settle in seated or laying positions on an earthen floor. Usually, several hot rocks are introduced as well as water that has been prepared with medicinal plants. It takes about two hours and requires great concentration due to the temperatures, darkness, steam, and the process of considering the cycle of life and death throughout the experience. I (Kasun) had worked with a spiritual guide in the past with students in a similar informal fashion. I had selected this guide because he was recommended by Martha Mata of CILAC Freire and because she had done her first sweat with him in the temazcal several years prior. She sensed he was faithful to all she had learned about temazcal healing practices and sensitive to the needs of the participants.

As we gathered outside on the patio next to the adobe temazcal, the spiritual guide asked each of us to set an intention during the ritual. Ricardo set his intention for the ritual, 'to leave the temazcal a better person than I was when I entered'. After cleansing with water, each of us entered the dark cave-like structure with the only light coming from the opening. There was intense heat coming from the stones in the center. As we sat next to each other in a semicircle, our bodies physically touching, the entrance was closed and we were surrounded by complete darkness. Silvia recalled her experience during the temazcal ritual:

> I was terrified to say the least. I have allowed fear to control my life for several years now and it has infiltrated every crevice of my daily being. Once the door was closed and the hole on top was covered, we were deprived of all visual sense...Like meditation, I was forced to think

Figure 3.1 Temazcal/sweat lodge space. Photo by Marks, author.

about things. To this day, I find myself going back inside that Temazcal internally and what happened in there. I would say that I wanted to stop relying on the opinion of others because this is where most of my fears in life come from.

Silvia described the temazcal ritual and the impact the experience had on her psyche to heal self-doubt and overcome fears prohibiting her from living the life she wanted to live.

Reflecting on their lived experiences and personal knowledge in the temazcal, the Latinx students reflected inward toward their own healing. Lupe anticipated a deep connection with her culture, ancestors, and herself as she entered the temazcal. During the ritual, she felt a wholeness to her past and present:

I blamed my Mexican origins for my spiritual connections, as I grew up with stories about curses and spirits, I naturally assumed this connection with being Mexican. I now believe that it is through this indigenous ancestry that I am able to connect so deeply with the world around me and therefore, live my life with these connections as my ancestors did. That's why, when going to the Temazcal, I had no doubts that it would make some sort of impact on my life.

The heat felt like it was opening me up spiritually, allowing space for realizations. I was feeling all sorts of energies and feelings I didn't know existed that I wanted to keep feeling. ... was able to clearly see my whole essence. The temazcal gave me clarity but even weeks after it happened, I've still felt weightless and more content with my overall life.

Lupe's reflection after the experience shows her reintegration of ancestors, recognitions of colonized versions of her people's past, and her sense of self as more integrated than prior to entry into the temazcal. This experience was pivotal for the group, even for the one student who was unable to attend, and we underscored it to show the profundity of personal and communal work the program held space for. We turn now to several thematic understandings of how the students engaged the curriculum in order that the reader might see threads of what is possible on the larger scale for what happens when Latinx students are centered in the program.

Personal Story as Creation of Agency

The primary purpose of testimonials is to foreground personal experiences within social circumstances so as to describe a person's struggles as minoritized people in a White-dominant society and place them into the historical consciousness (Mohanty, 2003). The methodological approach of testimonio has roots in the struggles of people who have experienced inequities and persecution in Latin America (Delgado Bernal et al., 2012). Delgado Bernal et al. explain testimonio 'incorporates political, social, historical, and cultural histories that accompany one's life experiences as a means to bring about change through consciousness changing' (p. 364). In the program, it was important to hear one another's stories and listen to how each person handled their struggles with agency. By storytelling, the Latinx students raised consciousness about their lived experiences as Latinx people in the Global North.

Students expressed how being and interconnecting in the spaces within Mexico made them confront and disrupt their own thinking toward a new way of interconnecting with people and places. For instance, during a class session, Lupe transformed her knowledge and thinking during the study abroad program as she exclaimed, 'How can I live my life in a way that shows how much I've changed on this trip?' Carlos expressed the evolution of his thoughts and feelings about himself and people in the Global South with the following statement, 'I have a new diverse look on life. I just might have to change my perspective. I know for a fact I will take the things I learned here with me and use them in my daily life back in [city]'. Oscar had a similar revelation as Carlos when he wrote, 'Once you learn something it changes your perspective on life, you can't go back'. Ricardo believed his unlearning of Eurocentric education and relearning of his own history and heritage was a significant change within him as he asked, 'How can I take everything that I've learned and the experience here and apply this to my life living in the U.S.?' These are impactful statements about the Latinx students' perspective to be change agents in their own lives.

Silvia wrote her truths about marginalized people within the dominant culture as she reflected, 'I feel like this is a way of knowing that many people of color and ethnic minorities develop during their life because of the systemic injustices and marginalization that forces them to grapple with the multiplicity of truths. We had knowledge about operating in one culture and operating in the other various cultures that we were a part of'. The need for the Latinx students to conform to mainstream culture manifests as a fluid identity (Keating, 2013). These lived experiences of the Latinx students are not our own experiences as White women or a Latinx man a generation older, so, we reflected deeply to their testimonials about their lives. Some discussions led to profound dialogue by the Latinx students.

During one of our class discussions, Kasun discussed the concept of pobrecito (poor thing) and the scholar, Eugene Garcia (2001), who wrote about pobrecito syndrome, which is when U.S. teachers focus on a deficit ideology and view Latinx children as lacking while ignoring the strengths of the children. *Pobrecito* invites lower expectations and a sense of charity as opposed to authentic relationships based in reciprocity. When teachers manifest a sense of charity toward Latinx communities, this becomes problematic in schools as they lower expectations of Latinx students as a result. If a person takes a patronizing attitude toward others, they do not imagine them as possessing authority and ownership of their lives.

Antonio, a visiting Mexican faculty member who at the time taught at a U.S. university (and a close friend of Kasun) and had participated for several days with the students, reflected with the group. He explained the way the Indigenously oriented alternative school, a space that provided life lessons and community in a very economically poor part of the city (described in greater detail in Chapter 4), was breaking the charity paradigm:

The church ladies that came with their gifts for Christmas. And instead of… There's always a risk of being scrutinized because you can be perceived as…ungrateful, right? 'What? How can you like do that to me? How can you tell me that you are not going to receive gifts from me?

Obviously you need them.' And for them to be like: 'no, that's not how we work. This is what we're trying to do.' And then breaking that cycle; I think it takes a lot of courage because you don't know how society is going to scrutinize you. You don't know how these organizations are going to scrutinize you. To rich people. Right? They feel like what they're doing is good and so changing or breaking the charity paradigm. It's great that they're able to.

Lupe connected with the idea of pobrecito syndrome in her own experiences and told her own story:

So I live in trailer parks. So constantly there is churches that come to our neighborhood. Like we love the free stuff, trust me, but it's kind of insulting that over the summer they provide meals because they think none of us have food. There definitely are some people who do struggle with hunger but I don't think going to a trailer park in one county is necessarily the best place to tackle hunger. And it's like, every summer they'll have people coming over here with sandwiches. It's kind of sometimes my parents will just take us. But it's showing your face there. Oh, like: 'you're here, you're accepting the free food because you need it, because you guys don't have food over the summer.'

And what we needed are our kids to keep being in school. Our dropout rate was in our, my neighborhood was through the roof. I think my graduating class was like the biggest graduating class from that whole neighborhood. And like the past 10 years. And that says a lot because it was like five of us. And it just goes to show you, what we needed were tutors and now we have them. And now we're seeing better things, but it was like, we don't need sandwiches that just have ham and cheese and the little mustard, mayo packets, like really.

Silvia connected with what Lupe was saying and built on the idea of pobrecito syndrome by adding her own understanding in the following: 'And I was going to say that a lot of charity work it comes from signs of like a hero complex. The sense of like "I'm going to save you rather than asking what you need." So, it comes from a place of "I'm going to be selfish and I'm going to help you"'. Due to neoliberal structures, people perpetuate these feelings of charity and make it comfortable for people to have hero complexes and not ever know the real people they are 'helping' or build relationships. Is it colonizing for people who initiate charity to make the less advantaged feel even more less than? Using this discussion of charity, we gained an understanding about the lives of the community in Mexico and the lived experiences of people in our own study abroad group. As the Latinx students encountered unjust power structures, we focused on using a critical and compassionate lens. The study abroad program provided a space to understand the complexities of the lives of the people in Mexico and for the Latinx students to examine their own lived experiences. As the Latinx students critically looked at 'common differences', they formed solidarity with the people in the local community. Through solidarity, they moved forward by connecting through their commonalities, not forgetting their individual critical differences (Keating, 2013).

The solidarity felt among group members allowed for a communal reflection on students' U.S. K-12 schooling. This program's curriculum intentionally confronted inaccuracies learned in school so the Latinx students could rewrite what they have learned in Global North schools. Such confrontations occurred in the literature read before departure and then in Mexico from thought leaders during chats about social movements (e.g. Zapatismo and Mexican feminism) as well as through the language instructors at CILAC Freire. The Latinx students challenged their missing and erased heritage and history through Eurocentric education. The goal was not to replace Western knowledge but to integrate Latinx and Indigenous knowledge systems (Keating, 2013). Rewriting history is a form of resistance and agency as we moved to the forefront of subjugated knowledge of marginalized people.

Finding Familiar Context in U.S. Education

Eurocentric ideology and epistemology were a common lived experience by the Latinx students within their schooling in the United States. The new knowledge gained during the study abroad program in Mexico was in opposition to the hegemonic discourses learned in the United States. These discourses they encountered in school centered around stories and history of the dominant group ignoring the culture and heritage of the Latinx students. In Kasun and Lee's (2017) study of transnational Mexican-origin families, Kasun wrote, 'Most students agreed that it never seemed to occur to teachers to ask them about their expertise about Mexico when discussing social studies, literature, or any curricular material' (p. 135). While in the Global South, the Latinx students gained knowledge and pride in their own heritage and history. Ana reflected on the lack of historical context and cultural relevance of her education:

> It wasn't until coming to Teotihuacan that I truly realized that [Local state history] is not mine. The history I've been taught in school has truly been irrelevant to my culture, my heritage and the experiences they have lived. This, Teotihuacan, was relevant to me and my culture, but I had to be 20 and out [of] the country to be catered to in my pursuit of education...I would have appreciated knowing where I came from earlier in life.

Jimena described her experience in school and the overwhelming White dominance she experienced:

> The culture I had at home did not fit in with my school life and what was talked about in school, it was my own little world. I did not have a teacher understand my culture and customs. I could not learn about physical and chemical changes in science class by the example of making s'mores. I had never had them.

Both Ana and Jimena were aware of the lack of Latinx experiences, history, and culture present in U.S. schools. They felt a lack of connection and relevance in their U.S. education.

Lupe, Jimena, and Silvia were educated in schools in the United States and each of them experienced deficit beliefs about Latinx students from the system. Deficit thinking blames inequality on a lack of intellectual abilities and an absence of values on a group of people and not on the oppression emanating from inequities and lack of power within the system (Gorski, 2008; Yosso, 2005). Lupe described her frustration with the low expectations in U.S. schools, 'I definitely felt misunderstood because I was always underestimated by my own teachers'. Jimena had a similar experience in school when she said, 'I was usually the only Latina in advanced classes while the other Latinos were all together in the lower classes and ESOL classes'. Silvia depicted her negative experience in school in the southern United States as being, 'most hurtful, being praised for not being like the other Hispanic kids because I was smart and spoke English fluently'. She described an incident in her U.S. school with a teacher that lacked knowledge and empathy, 'I asked an English teacher why there was not any literature made by Hispanics. She answered that there just wasn't any and that there were no great Hispanic writers in the United States. Imagine my surprise when I discovered Anzaldua's work'. The lack of competency of this teacher was hurtful to the identity of Silvia. Each of these Latinx students had school experiences in the Global North where teachers and schools had low expectations and a lack of cultural understanding of Latinx students. These negative experiences in U.S. schools contributed to commonalities among these four Latinx students creating a connection between them.

The Latinx students' educational experiences in the Global North intensified their feelings of marginalization within the system. In contrast, the Latinx students experienced community and love within the Indigenous-focused alternative school based on Don Miguel Ruiz's (1997) *Four Agreements*. The cultural space in the Indigenous alternative school in Mexico was viewed by the Latinx students as communal and collective which diverged from their lived experiences of individualism represented in Western culture. Ana experienced this space of cultural dissonance while feeling a sense of community at the Indigenous alternative school. She described her experience of connecting her own learning in the United States with her learning experience with the students in the Indigenous alternative school:

> Yeah. We each had a little square, each section and then every two minutes or so, we would have to rotate the next tile then the person that was taking over our tile would have to complete it. At the end of whatever the section, it would have been five people working on each tile. [T]he woman told us that it was to promote creativity and different ways of thinking. Because I might have one idea and then the other student goes and picks up where I left off and have a different idea based on what I had already going on. I'm not going to complete that vision either because the next person is going to see both of our works and have a different vision completely…Nothing is mine, everything is ours.

Figure 3.2 Collaborative art work completed by youth participants and adult guides in Caminando Unidos and participants of the program. Photo by Marks, author.

To work collectively, the students at the school had to have trust in one another as they each worked to do their best. One of the Toltec's four agreements was 'Always do your best' (Ruiz, 1997). Ruiz described this agreement as 'you are going to be productive, you are going to be good to yourself, because you will be giving yourself to your family, to your community, to everything' (p. 78). In one of Ana's reflections, she wrote, 'Hispanic cultures are way more collective in their mindset than American cultures. We see people in Mexico operating in the collective where these values are rooted in Indigenous beliefs such as the *Four Agreements* (Ruiz, 1997)'. During one of our class discussions, we defined the term *communal* as the way people share in a community which was different than *solidarios*. We talked about how there was no word in English that closely represents solidarios. Our construction of the meaning of solidarios was described as being a commitment to working together and helping each other.

Solidarios was built within the Indigenous alternative school by creating an environment where students freely expressed their feelings. Lupe saw differences in the expression of emotions between schools in the Global North and the Indigenous alternative school. This experience in the study abroad program made Lupe feel regret about her own school background which lacked emotional support:

> And I wrote about kind of how I wish I would've have received some kind of emotional support like that in school. Imagine how much more competent we would all be in facing our own emotions. And whenever things get too hard and how we're so hard on ourselves. It's kind of makes you like retrospect and we think, this could have been. It's good that they're receiving it because now that we're exposed to it, we can teach our own children that as well. But now that I'm witnessing and I'm like, 'Wow, like I really wish that.'

What she witnessed was a school with a coherent set of beliefs that guide behavior through mindfulness and gratitude. Oscar noticed the difference in Western and Indigenous education systems with this statement, 'the emotional aspect is missing in our systems of education in the U.S.' The Latinx students believed in the importance of acknowledging and supporting emotions in schools. The juxtaposition of the individualistic, cognitive orientation of education in the United States contrasted with the collaborative, caring education observed in the Indigenous alternative school in Mexico. The Latinx students perceived the need for caring and support in education carried over into acknowledging and encouraging their abilities in Spanish language.

Healing through Self-Compassion

Healing was an act of acknowledging and accepting the humanity of each other and within ourselves. By openly sharing their personal feelings of oppression and marginalization, the Latinx students began to replace these feelings with self-compassion. The act of compassion is to be open and present (Brown, 2008); it requires a stance of kindness and generosity. Compassion can be decolonial in its sense of empathy, its ability to be forgiving, if not also non-judgmental. In a continually colonizing world, punishment, judgment, and 'success' are stronger drivers than the slow work of compassion. In a world in dire need of healing, compassion is a stronger goal and mode of being if we want to bring ourselves back together.

The discussion of compassion during our second class in Mexico organically formed from learning the Toltec Four Agreements. Discussion of compassion centered on the Toltec agreement 'Don't take anything personally'. The conversation started with defining the term 'compassion' with the students sharing personal examples during class discussion. While Kasun had touchstone ideas and concepts she wanted to engage during the in-Mexico experience, she also left space for the students to shape the directions of the conversations, leaning into their insights, epiphanies, and lived experiences. Celia explained that compassion is not taking it personally when someone has hurt you. For example, someone coming from a dark space and this manifests itself by hurting someone else. Having compassion looks at this bruised person and sees a chance in some minimal way to help them be less bruised. This idea furthered the discussion of being available to people who hurt other people because they are displaying aspects of being bruised themselves. The example of compassion formed by the class exemplified the Toltec ideology. The faculty advisor guided us to the conclusion that it is hard to be compassionate with others if you do not like yourself or have self-compassion. Self-compassion was described by the Latinx students as allowing yourself to fail, following passions that make a person happy, understanding that everyone makes mistakes, and loving your imperfections.

To feel whole, the Latinx students transformed their feelings of cultural marginalization toward freely being able to express themselves. Climbing the stone trail toward the Tepozteco pyramid, Lupe realized an inner sense of self while being in Mexico as she stood on the clifftop:

> It was a personal goal that I had set to myself, to not let my fears get in the way of enjoying the beautiful view Tepoztlan had provided for me. I felt that I was really connected to myself.

Tepoztlan is a sacred place made significant by the local people through their relationship with the place and land. The local Indigenous people integrate their pre-Hispanic past, daily life, and community identity with mountains, trees, plants, animals, and common spaces creating a magical place, if not also contested. Mexico City residents descend in the hundreds of thousands to the town for weekend getaways, not more than 90 minutes from one of the world's largest cities. Enormous wealth from the outside has led to local struggles wherein the locals have succeeded in keeping major food and hotel chains out of their town in order to help preserve its local heritage. The local community's respect and reciprocity with place was evident to the Latinx students as they interacted with this sacred place in situ both visually and physically. The resiliency and history of the community and place was shared with everyone during the experience while the Latinx students encountered a community's collective being and resistance to commercialization.

This ethos of resistance to colonial forces created the ability to 'study within' by the Latinx students and allowed them to be their own person. The connection to sacred place contrasts with the U.S. detachment in maintaining cultural and sacred places. The intention of a sacred space throughout Tepoztlan brought forth a sense of history and feelings of convivir among the local community while connecting the Latinx students to the land and the people in the community.

Hiking the steep trail at an altitude of 5,600 feet to the top of the mountain, the study abroad students stuck together to support and encourage each other. Along the trail, we stopped at a shady point along the cliff to let others catch up and share snacks. The hike up took about 90 minutes, 2 hours for some. Walking up and over the rocks, someone was always willing to lend their hand to pull another up. The physical ascent of Tepoztlan was not only an individual accomplishment but a group experience. The term 'we' was used by many of the Latinx students to describe the experience of reaching the summit. The journey up the mountain was a collective experience as everyone took care of each other throughout the climb up the mountain and demonstrated compassion for everyone's unique attributes, from perceived weaknesses to skills.

Walking through Tepoztlan, Ana was impacted by the image of hummingbirds and paused to think, 'The colibri [hummingbird] to me symbolizes living in the now, being present on the moment and giving yourself a moment to enjoy'. Each moment for Ana was an act of self-compassion. These revelations were so significant for her that she had an image of a hummingbird tattooed on her when she was back in the United States.

We revisit the temazcal as another point of entry for understanding how compassion was formed among the students. After the temazcal ritual, many of the students felt more emotional. In class we talked about how the experience of the temazcal was an act of compassion. We needed to have self-compassion for the areas we decided to focus on physically and emotionally. During class, several students shared what they were thinking about during the temazcal and we discussed their feelings of guilt of being on this study abroad program when family and friends could not cross the border. As the students talked about their guilt, they confronted the reality that guilt does not go away and it is not productive. Expressing feelings of compassion and empathy for those who cannot come to Mexico was more productive.

Ana discovered her feelings of connectivity to the people and place of Mexico and found the ability to have self-compassion:

> I can't say I found myself in Mexico, but I certainly found bits and pieces to take back and reclaim as my own. One can only hope to reclaim enough to feel whole again. The temazcal showed me an image of myself shattered into pieces—I think I've been able to piece back together.

There are several moments within the program where Ana was introspective and examined her lived experiences in the Global North and her connections to her heritage in Mexico. These deep emotions came to light as each of us shared and became more visible to each other.

To heal, the Latinx students became inclusive with each other by sharing feelings and personal experiences within the group. Lupe said, 'I don't feel like I'm the same person that came in'. This realization was related to the context of the place and the people she was surrounded by in the study abroad program. She had trepidation that the feelings she had while in Mexico would not carry over when she returned to the United States. She acknowledged that home (Global North) is not the same environment she experienced in Mexico (Global South).

Difficulty and Joy of Building Relationships

Going on a study abroad program involved a certain level of personal risk by the study abroad students. Several students mentioned their feelings about taking risks during the program and being open-minded to new experiences. Ricardo wrote in his reflection, 'I came to Mexico with an open mind, ready to soak up all of the knowledge and experience I could from a country that was beautiful yet foreign to me'. Being willing to listen with an open mind, the Latinx students crossed cultural boundaries as they connected with others in the group and the local community. Ana described her feelings of being unsettled as she opened herself to new experiences, 'Many lines, barriers, and boundaries were suspended in the last two weeks, and not in a bad way'. Eva wrote, 'The program pushed us to think critically and move away from our previous social schemes, norms, and notions about reality'. As we connected with each other, we disrupted feelings of silence and isolation by openly sharing lived experiences with empathy toward others. By listening and acknowledging the feelings of each other, we conferred worth to each other's experiences as we created relationships.

Through empathy, people build meaningful and trusting relationships. The environment for creating a community with empathy meant listening with an open heart and without judgment. Silvia commented, 'Being able to hold or accept multiple truths while having my own obvious interpretation has enabled me to have empathy and compassion for the ways of knowing of others'.

Being in Mexico brought forth physical feelings of being a part of somewhere without judgment. Carlos articulated his feelings of inclusion by interpreting a drawing he had created:

> I portrayed what I've been talking about the whole time that I've been here, which is how I feel comfortable speaking languages and being myself without feeling judged. So, I put a road in there, put three very diverse people, curly hair, bald and super short. One's saying 'Hola' and then one below and saying 'Bonjour' smiling and throwing like rays of sunshine because everybody's wanting the same road, but they're not feeling judged. And they feel like they can be their own person.

Carlos' description of his visual represented the comradery and solidarity he was feeling in Mexico while recognizing our individual differences.

Silvia described how she confronted her own initial fears of participating in the program, 'I'm afraid of not connecting. And the key point being the connection, not finding the connection'. Ana felt the same way as she admitted her fears to entering a situation where she did not know anyone, while stating this out loud took courage. Carlos exposed his own insecurities with participating in the group as he stated, 'I feel like I never put in something of value compared to what others are putting in'. With each of these testimonials, the others in the program demonstrated empathy through supportive comments and outright physical embodiments of empathy such as clapping and crying. Thich Nhat Hanh (2013) said, 'Compassionate communication is an extraordinarily powerful way to create mutual understanding and make changes' (p. 110). Silvia, Ana, and Carlos overcame their fears and connected with each other and others in the group. Along with the Latinx students, the faculty for the program took risks as they spoke personally from a vulnerable space and shared personal stories. From the beginning of the program, we examined within ourselves why we had been resistant in the past to being open.

The ability for us to be vulnerable in the study abroad program was an act of being courageous. We talked through moving beyond personal fears and self-doubt. For some of the Latinx students, the process of applying and coming on the trip was a form of vulnerability. Allowing for vulnerability, the Latinx students were able to fully participate in all of the experiences in the study abroad program. Living life is full of risks, and fully living involves being vulnerable (Ruiz, 1997).

In any group dynamic, the feelings of vulnerability are present as people in the group determine how much of themselves they want to share (Brantmeier, 2013). To be vulnerable, a person risks opening themselves to others and possible emotional stress. In a classroom, becoming vulnerable is an emotional experience. When acceptance, trust, and relational connections are created in the space of a classroom, the students are more willing to openly share and reflect on what they are hearing from others and their own feelings. By sharing their life experiences, the Latinx students connected with each other and their personal stories resonated with others in the group. As someone spoke their truth or became vulnerable, another person spoke up and empathized with the other person. The feelings of connection between the study abroad group was evident in the interactions and feelings expressed throughout the program. Lupe wrote, 'A traditional classroom setting couldn't have provided us with the ability to all connect and be comfortable showing each other our vulnerabilities in the way this study abroad did'. Ana felt deep connections to 'unlikely friends' as she expressed, 'I wanted to know them forever, but I guess that's what happens when you feel safe'. The trust built within the study abroad group was based on compassion, nonjudgment, and empathy. Carlos expressed:

> Being here in Mexico has given me an opportunity to fit in. At the beginning of the trip I felt like there was nothing that I could contribute but I realized that, whether it is something as simple as translating or walking one of the girls home I am contributing. I feel like here in Mexico I was able to open up quickly with our [university] family and that is something that rarely happens with me. I am able to share about my sexuality and depressive past without feeling judged or scared and that is something I will forever remember after we leave this trip.

The ability to overcome the risk of being vulnerable was difficult, although all the study abroad students contributed openly in class discussions, which encouraged the group to develop a relational bond and forge a community.

These relational bonds extended to the teachers at CILAC Freire, where the Latinx students felt a welcoming and warm environment which supported learning together. Ana explained, 'It wasn't always about speaking, sometimes listening to others say exactly what you felt meant more'. While Ricardo said, 'The staff members at [CILAC Freire] were wonderful and very friendly, I enjoyed being around and taught by them'. Eva reflected on the connections she made with other students during lessons at the Spanish language school:

> It is interesting to observe how in our group language has helped us establish relationships with our ever-changing identities, allowing us to complement each other and feel vulnerable without being judged. Language has allowed us to unite and contrast our identities in a way that is personal to each, but also doing this in recognized groups spaces. For most of us, it is a common link that breaks through barriers and makes us feel part of a community, it unites us, it allows us to understand each other in ways that are different and separate from our daily routine.

Eva indicated the idea of unity and community during her experiences at the Spanish language school within her reflection. In the Spanish language school, the Latinx students developed relationships with each other and the teachers. Each class discussion involved opening up and sharing personal stories that touched on social justice issues in the local community. The give-and-take interactions between the Cilac Freire teachers and study abroad students provided context for situated differences and connections through intersectionality.

However, it was the students within the group who developed the deepest connections. Carlos wrote about everyone in the group, 'I experienced such good vibes and thoughts that I never expected to experience'. Lupe reflects on a photo:

> This is one of my favorite pictures from the trip. This picture shows a few of us resting, preparing ourselves to keep climbing to the top of the mountain. This was taken a week after we climbed Teotihuacan, where a lot of the pictures I took were just of me. Now, I was taking pictures of people where we were in a vulnerable state, but at least we were there together. It was just incredibly beautiful looking at this picture, seeing the contrast from a week ago where most of us wouldn't have climbed this together as a group. It shows the growth we had in that short week and how we had bonded to a point where we wouldn't have in a traditional classroom setting. A traditional classroom setting couldn't have provided us with the ability to all connect and be comfortable showing each other our vulnerabilities in the way this study abroad did, and it was why I took this picture to be reminded of how close we all got in a short time.

During class, feelings of inclusion were prominent in the spaces of our class meetings. Silvia wrote in her caption under a picture of all of us sitting in a circle around a large firepit while in the class meeting at the faculty director's home, 'This was a very cathartic class and it allowed [us] to reflect a lot about our lives'. In her terminology, she used 'we' and 'our' as she talks about the class. This was no longer an individual reflection but a collective reflection inclusive of all of us. Ana wrote, 'I am surrounded by people who feel like me. I'm dreading leaving here, because I know the moment I leave this group of people and this place [I] will go back to being stuck'. The development of friendships, relationships, and community impacted the Latinx students. Celia asked the question, 'Why did I feel the need to hide how I really felt before?' This question and Ana's statement revealed how lived experiences in the United States lack outwardly expressed emotions and a lack of vulnerability with others. Ana and Celia described the lack of connections made within the United States because people do not reveal their true selves and speak from the heart. Celia then asked the question, 'How can I voice my own thoughts and concerns more actively in my community?' She wanted to connect with others in her community in the United States to raise consciousness. Through the decolonizing pedagogy of collective learning, the Latinx students transformed their ways of thinking about themselves and their community by aspiring to change their lives and their community in the United States.

References

Anzaldúa, G. (1981). Acts of healing. In C. Moraga & G. Anzaldúa (Eds.), *This bridge called my back: Writings by radical women*. New York: SUNY Press.
Brantmeier, E.J. (2013). Pedagogy of vulnerability: Definitions, assumptions and applications. In J. Lin, R.L. Oxford, & E.J. Brantmeier (Eds.), *Re-envisioning higher education: Embodied pathways to wisdom and social transformation* (pp. 96–106). Information Age.
Brown, B. (2008). *I thought it was just me (but it isn't): Making the journey from "What will people think" to "I am enough"*. New York: Avery.
Cajete, G. (2000). Indigenous knowledge: The pueblo metaphor of indigenous education. In M. Battiste (Ed.), *Reclaiming indigenous voice and vision* (pp. 181–191). Vancouver, Canada: UBC Press.
Delgado Bernal, D., Burciaga, R., & Flores Carmona, J. (2012). Chicana/Latina testimonios: Mapping the methodological, pedagogical, and political. *Equity & Excellence in Education*, *45*(3), 363–372.
Four Arrows (2016). *Point of departure: Returning to our more authentic worldview for education and survival*. Charlotte, NC: Information Age Publishing, Inc.
Garcia, E. (2001). *Hispanic education in the United States: Raíces y alas*. Lanham: Rowman & Littlefield Publishers, Inc.
Gorski, P. (2008). Good intentions are not enough: A decolonizing intercultural education. *Intercultural Education*, *19*(6), 515–525. https://doi.org/10.1080/14675980802568319
Kasun, G. S., & Lee, H. (2017). From "blissfully unaware" to "another perspective on hope": An indigenous knowledge study abroad program's impacts on the ways of knowing of pre-service transnational English learner teachers. *Teacher Education & Practice*, *30*(3), 425–442.

Keating, A. (2013). *Transformation now! toward a post-oppositional politics of change*. Urbana, Il.: University of Illinois Press.
Kimmerer, R. (2013). *Braiding sweetgrass: Indigenous wisdom, scientific knowledge, and the teachings of plants*. Canada: Milkweed Editions.
Mohanty, C. T. (2003). *Feminism without borders: Decolonizing theory, practicing solidarity*. Durham, NC: Duke University Press.
Nhat Hanh, T. (2013). *The art of communicating*. New York: HarperOne.
Ruiz, D. M. (1997). *The four agreements: A Toltec wisdom book*. San Rafael, CA: Amber-Allen.
Saavedra, C. & Nymark, E. (2008). Borderland-Mestizaje feminism: The new tribalism. In N. K. Denzin, Y. S. Lincoln, & L. T. Smith (Eds.), *Handbook of critical and indigenous methodologies* (pp. 255–276). Los Angeles, CA: Sage.
Yosso, T. (2005). Whose culture has capital? A critical race theory discussion of community cultural wealth. *Race Ethnicity and Education*, *8*(1), 69–91.

4 Collaborating with Local Partners and Communities

Through Shared Ownership

The chapter describes the decolonizing curriculum in the study abroad program, which involved collaborating with the local community by participating in an Indigenously oriented alternative school and a social-justice-oriented language school. The chapter also discusses the service learning experience, which allowed the Latinx students to connect deeply with the students and staff at the alternative school. The study abroad students and the local community formed solidarity by working in collective ways to initiate agency against oppressive systems. The authors conclude with a discussion on the need to articulate the perspectives and thoughts of the local community in study abroad programs, as research has often neglected the voices of the host communities.

Centering the Decolonial in Local Partnerships

In recognition of the power dynamics of working in spaces that are less resourced than the 50 U.S. states where we reside, we explore our efforts of creating dialogic and caring relationships with our host partners within Mexico. This includes open recognition of the colonial condition between our territories as well as our earnest efforts to decolonize our programming. For instance, we show the uniquely situated stories of relationships that often predated our initial contacts with trusted friends in networks of activists. The relationships formed in the study abroad program and the local community created connections of care and built trust. Creating activities in the local community provided opportunities to learn beyond the classroom and form alliances with others who also live with the historical effects of colonization. Experiential activities impacted the perception of the students on the economic situations in Latin American countries and how they experienced similar but different spaces in the United States. Living and experiencing daily/routines in the social-justice-oriented language school, CILAC Freire, an Indigenously oriented alternative school, Caminando Unidos, and homestays elicited feelings of

DOI: 10.4324/9781003320111-5

connectedness to the people and place. Acknowledging differences, our host partners and students did not view socioeconomic or cultural differences as barriers to forming strong affective connections.

The decolonizing curriculum in the study abroad program provided collaborations with the local community by participating in CILAC Freire and service learning in Caminando Unidos. During the study abroad program, CILAC Freire served as a communal place to meet the homestay families, deepen connection to heritage language, and learn from community activists. The give-and-take interactions between the teachers at CILAC Freire and the students during the conversations in language classes elicited feelings of connectedness. Each participant in the discussion became open and vulnerable as they delved into conversations about social justice issues in local communities in Mexico. Other curricular moments involved interweaving local cultural issues into the program through charlas/testimonials by local activists. During the charlas, the students political consciousness was raised by the significance of colonization on both sides of the border as it divides and oppresses people who were not White.

The service learning experience at Caminando Unidos elicited intense feelings of connectedness. Through empathy, the Latinx students constructed a deeper understanding and deeper connection with students and staff throughout the experience at the school (Brown, 2008). David Peat (2002) stated, 'The best one can hope is to open your mind to see the world as they see it' (p. 50). The Latinx students expressed the dichotomy they felt between the idea of community within Caminando Unidos and the lack of community they perceive in the United States. One student stated, 'It's not about being better than the next, but using what you have to uplift the rest'. The lived values of hospitality and care was embedded within the culture of the school, as students expressed they felt 'being welcomed into a family that had so much joy and love to give'. The relational approach in the curricula and community of the school permitted each of the study abroad participants to learn and connect with the students and staff.

During interviews, the students and host families revealed relationships within the homestay experience as they acknowledged the mutual care and respect toward each other. Familial ties developed between the host families and study abroad students for the brief time they spent together. The communal meals from the homestay families initiated conversations and initiated a reciprocal relationship during the experience.

Through relationships and thoughtful participation, the Latinx students and the local community formed solidarity by working in collective ways to initiate agency against oppressive systems (Mohanty, 2003). Mohanty suggested, 'Agency is thus figured in the small, day-to-day practices and struggles' which address issues of identity and communities such as home and family (p. 83). The practice of telling personal stories through testimonios and rewriting history to counter the hegemonic narrative present in the United States 'leads to the formation of politicized consciousness and self-identity' (Mohanty, 2003, p. 78). Anzaldúa (2002) said, 'Where before we saw only separateness, differences, and polarities, our connectionist sense of spirit recognizes nurturance and reciprocity and encourages alliances among groups working to transform communities' (p. 568). The curriculum, experiences, and interactions in the study abroad program raised critical consciousness by being emotionally affected by unjust global realities. Solidarity among the Latinx students and with the local community crossed borders to work toward social change. Jimena said, 'I have learned that it is important to be informed but even more important to be part of the change you want to see'. Essential connections between the study abroad students created a space where we were our whole selves with our own voices, experiences, culture, and languages coming together and forming a community.

Creating Critical Consciousness with the Local Community

How can we continue the efforts of solidarity to promote community activism and connections to the host community with mutual benefit and reciprocity? Lacking in the research is the articulation of the perspectives and thoughts of the local community (Hartman et al., 2020: Pirbhai Illich & Martin, 2019). Research on Global North and Global South immersion and study abroad programs has lacked more than one perspective as 'voices of host communities in such studies have been silenced or, if included in the study, have been interpreted by those who use a mainstream lens' (Pirbhai Illich & Martin, 2019, p. 68). To fully engage study abroad students by reducing barriers and connecting with local communities, the content within the study abroad program needs to make visible the impact of colonization and create beneficial collaborations (Hartman et al., 2020). Programs need to decolonize sources of knowledge through personal stories, critical conversations, and diverse local community testimonials. Study abroad faculty need to look for opportunities to connect to social activists along with social justice and human rights organizations within the host community.

Study abroad programming needs to be examined to see where students connect to local communities and on what level they connect. There were several points of connection with the local community during this study abroad program. In the findings, the Latinx students reflected on relationships they built with the teachers at CILAC Freire, the students at Caminando Unidos, and their homestay families. Through the relational approach of this study, the study abroad students and host country connected with profound dialogue which was decolonizing through the gains in understanding and empathy. Deeper engagement with host communities should be encouraged to provide opportunities to raise consciousness between the students and host country. The connectivity between study abroad programs and host countries can be further investigated to reveal opportunities for collaborations and collective actions between the students and local community members. Relational approaches can shift the conversation from walls between the United States and Mexico toward bridges. We provide a snapshot of the kind of relational and pedagogical work CILAC Freire does with the students we have brought them in the following example.

During the first week of the study abroad program, the director of CILAC Freire, Martha Mata, guided us in a curricular experience at the downtown municipal mercado. This market was first established in 1964, housing hundreds of stalls that provide fresh food, plastic and metalware goods, herbs, spices, and traditional remedies including statues of saints and other forms of ancient traditional herbal healing mixtures.

Figure 4.1 Cuernavaca Municipal Market. Photo by Marks, author.

A massive cement dome covers the main part of the market. A central meeting point where we gathered is referred to as 'La Virgen', a large, electrically illuminated statue of the Lady of Guadalupe where locals offer fresh bouquets of flowers. Not unlike other large markets in Mexico, it is full of regional produce, colors spanning the rainbow, meats, fish, cheeses, handicrafts of all colors, and materials. About 30,000 people shop there every day, Martha explained. This is an activity the school routinely offers to visitors and students, they said, to learn about the material realities of Mexico and to see how everyday Mexicans find the best prices to feed and take care of their families in what are commonly economically difficult circumstances. The experience also links the traditional Indigenous experience of bartering and exchanging goods and services to what is now a partially open-air market covering about five square city blocks. Typically, according to CILAC Freire, students either walk the 20 minutes to the market or take the city bus, the most common means of transportation for locals in Cuernavaca.

Gathering initially at the language school, we walked to the bus stop and boarded the local public bus to the downtown mercado. Martha explained, 'Most Mexicans take the local bus, so that's what we will also do, and imagine coming back with your arms loaded with all the things you will consider buying'. We arrived and walked through the serpentine food stalls outside the market to then gather in the large food section where there were rows of colorful food stalls piled high with yellow mangos, dragon fruits, deep orange papayas, red and white onions, cucumbers, oranges, and cilantro. We were divided into groups and each given a scenario to feed a family of four on two Mexican minimum wages. The scenario was hypothetical, but a powerful representation. Students spent an hour in a small group of four, guided by one of the teachers from CILAC Freire, considering what would stretch the furthest. They approached sellers at their respective stalls, 'How much for a kilo of corn tortillas? How much for a half kilo of beans? How much for a dozen eggs?' Then, among themselves, they discussed what they might feed their families. Suggestions ran from beef soup to eggs to rice and thoughts about nutrition to include fresh fruits and vegetables. They consulted each of the teachers about what they ate daily, about how the teachers would choose to feed their families, and how they stretch their own incomes over the years. The teachers openly engage and welcome these kinds of questions, showing that language instruction is always the twin skin of real-life activities, down to the core activities such as how to feed your family.

This class activity in the mercado had an impact on the perception of the students on the economic situations in Mexico and how these were similar but different spaces in the United States. Ricardo wrote about the activity at the mercado:

As a class, we did an activity where we separated into groups and went to the market with the task of buying food to supply a meal for a family of four. Thinking about how hard it is for someone to simply feed their family with the poor pay they receive in this country is heartbreaking.

While most of the students had faced economic hardships, none of them had struggled to feed an entire family.

The students privately, and then in our large class discussion, connected these struggles to their own stories and larger global economic ones. Ana realized the economic situation her parents must have faced in Mexico when she was participating in the mercado socioeconomic activity. Being in the physical place of the mercado, Ana reflected, 'At the mercado I found myself ... thinking about the circumstances my mom must have lived through that pushed her to leave was tough to process'. Ana gained a clear perspective of the hardship her mom faced before leaving her home in Mexico for a better life in the United States. The Latinx students struggled with the reality of the daily socioeconomics of life in Mexico and the options many people face, including their own family, to support a family. During class, we also connected to colonial dynamics from Mexico's history as a colonial country and its complicated relationship with the Global North country of the United States. While the dynamics of the border are not surmounted in one day, there are daily resistances the students discussed about 'getting ahead' for themselves and their families and working to improve conditions through mass actions like supporting the Dreamers program where youth brought to the United States without legal documents have found a (tenuous) pathway to limited legal participation in the U.S. work sector while waiting for a greater resolution to their statuses.

Local Community Partner: CILAC Freire

CILAC Freire (https://www.cilacfreire.mx/) was established over 30 years ago by Jorge Torres (who passed away in 2018) to provide a social-justice-oriented language institute for students from outside Mexico to learn advocacy work through language and a pedagogical approach mirroring Freire's ideas about consciousness-raising through literacy. For over ten years, I (Kasun) have worked with them and met activists and budding activists from all over the world, including Cesar Chavez's personal attorney, international leaders in bilingual education, and human rights activists from throughout the United States. While the school is physically small, it attracts individuals hungry for community and justice and delivers on those desires. While the school is now led by Torres's wife, Martha Mata, it maintains the same commitment to the community, to maintaining and living social justice values, and attracting collaborations and relationships from across the globe toward increasing justice in an ailing world. I spent a great deal of time visiting the couple and also hosting Torres while he was alive when he came to the United States to recruit students. Mata, Torres, and I presented on academic conference panels together about their connections as friends and collaborators. I note that there were (and still are at the time of press) many discussions with the school director about global inequality and education as well as sharing about the personal situations they face, from childrearing (Torres and Mata have one son while I have two children) to discussions about life goals and the meaning of our short times on this planet.

At CILAC Freire, the method for learning language is based on problem-posing. Problem-posing involves dialogue where the students and teacher are critical co-investigators who critically reflect to solve problems and enact change (Freire, 2000). They borrow their approach directly from Brazilian educator and theorist Paolo Freire (2000), whose work has inspired hundreds of millions the world over to name the world through the word in his innovative approach to literacy. Indeed, his approach was overtly political and an antidote to the traditional 'banking' approach to educational where teachers perceived their students as empty slates that could be 'filled' with knowledge. Instead, he believed learners had the tools at their disposal to name their realities and work toward improving them. As the Latinx students enthusiastically talked about their language classes in their heritage language, the elements of Freirian ideas emerged. The topics for language classes ranged from misogyny, religion, activism, and other relevant issues in Mexico (and beyond), and the dialogue provided a way to improve their linguistic abilities and gain different perspectives about the topics.

CILAC Freire has been committed to the community and its social justice principles since its inception over three decades ago, and this was an important attractor to Kasun when she established her relationship with them. Having been heavily influenced by Mexican advocates for social justice as an undergraduate during her own study abroad as a college student, she knew this approach would make all the difference for the kind of program she wanted to develop. In dialog over her first summer prior to offering the first program, CILAC Freire explained the kinds of activities that could be offered. Due to CILAC Freire's networks, a host of individuals and organizations could be visited with students. These ranged from more obvious tourist destinations such as the cathedral and historic downtown, but those more traditionally expected destinations would include a discussion of the famous Cuernavaca bishop who was a tireless advocate for justice and how the municipal palace in the town square is a site for regular protest of remembrance of those who have been disappeared or killed while advocating for justice. They are also able to offer programming that is only available due to trusted networks, such as access to the city's only all-Indigenous public school, a Mayan shaman, local activists involved in political struggles such as the LGBTQIA+ movement, and so on.

I (Kasun) note that I have routinely taken the role as learner with CILAC Freire despite my degrees or positioning as someone from the Global North. Indeed, I have been direct that she (Martha) understands I take students into Mexico because there are community-oriented solutions to global problems that do not yet exist in the United States. I have always had the language institute to develop their budget and then met the prices without hesitation, unless an activity would be too large for the overall budget. I have also let the school know, for instance, that my own students are working and first generation, usually, and that despite being from the United States, the students, too, are quite cost-sensitive. Well aware of Mexican pricing (for having lived there over several decades), I recognize the pricing offered has always been, in my understanding, more than fair. From my years of work with the school, I also know the school takes a very limited amount for overhead while paying providers exactly what I have been told. The transparency and dialog in this long-standing relationship have created the space for richer development of programming through the years.

CILAC Freire faculty continually evaluate programming with the participants in a collaborative effort to examine learning and build relationships. To encourage conviviality, an evaluation with the school faculty included a collective meal. Either before or after the meal, the school faculty discuss the impacts of the program with the students to determine the effectiveness of learning opportunities. During our final evaluation of the program, there was a ceremony and meal with the teachers at CILAC Freire and our homestay families. All the local food was prepared by our homestay families, which grounded the act of saying goodbye with warmth and hospitality. We were relaxed as we ate and talked with each other about the program and our experiences. After our meal, each homestay family presented a coffee mug and said some kind words about each of the students that stayed with them. These sentiments represented a connection with each student beyond the capitalist exchange of a bed and meals and allowed for acknowledgment of the relationships formed during the study abroad experience. The communal meal felt like being with family. Our collective experience created a sense of community. Through communal meals and authentic evaluation at CILAC Freire, the feelings of conviviality flourished.

CILAC Freire's sense of community and local activism was present from the moment everyone entered the doors of the Spanish language school in 2019. Warmth, hospitality, and commitment to community activism emanated from the bright, colorful Zapatista mural on one wall to the left of reproduced photos of Frida Kahlo. The classrooms were brightly painted with a large table and chairs, with each room named after Mexican activists. Upon entering through the front door, the stairs descended into an open and spacious room with large windows letting the light shine through and a comfortable sofa against one wall. This is where we gathered as a group to decompress from classes and one of the spaces for the academic classes. Toward the back wall was an open kitchen accessible to all, where we shared a refrigerator, coffee, tea, and other kitchen essentials. Shared spaces provided opportunities to casually interact with the CILAC Freire teachers and with each other.

In the language school, the Latinx students felt a welcoming and warm environment where the teachers and students supported learning together. Ana explained, 'It wasn't always about speaking sometimes listening to others say exactly what you felt meant more'. The teachers were expert at creating a safe space where exquisite attention was being paid to each student. The small class size and this reverence for each person's ideas created a broader impact where all class members took on the shared work of listening. While Ricardo said, 'The staff members at CILAC Freire were wonderful and very friendly, I enjoyed being around and taught by them'. Eva reflected on the connections she made with other students during lessons at the Spanish language school:

> It is interesting to observe how in our group language has helped us establish relationships with our ever-changing identities, allowing us to complement each other and feel vulnerable without being judged. Language has allowed us to unite and contrast our identities in a way that is personal to each, but also doing this in recognized groups spaces. For most of us, it is a common link that breaks through barriers and makes us feel part of a community, it unites us, it allows us to understand each other in ways that are different and separate from our daily routine.

Eva indicated the idea of unity and community during her experiences in the CILAC Freire classes within her reflection. In the Spanish language school, the Latinx students developed caring relationships with each other and the teachers. Each class discussion involved opening up and sharing personal stories that touched on social justice issues in the local community. The give-and-take interactions between the Spanish language teachers and study abroad students provided context for situated differences between the Global South and Global North and the connections made through intersectionality.

The Latinx students learned by engaging in meaningful and deliberate class discussions about the complex social realities in Mexico so they could understand issues such as immigration and transnationalism. In the curriculum of CILAC Freire, personal stories and cultural issues were interwoven into the course discussions. These personal stories and testimonials from local activists in the community were powerful ways to connect the study abroad students with the local community. The study abroad program was designed through a decolonial curriculum as a personal and collective journey.

Service Learning with Local Partners: Caminando Unidos

Starting in 1990, the organization Caminando Unidos (literally 'Walking Together') began addressing deep social needs of individuals who have lived in a context of exploitation, marginalization, few material resources, and violence. Individuals with training in social work from Mexico began addressing the deep needs, especially school-related ones (and then shortly thereafter the need for food and nutrition) of the nearby community. Many immigrants from other parts of Mexico, especially the more historically marginalized Indigenous areas where employment was exceedingly scarce, were relocating to unofficial housing on the sides of the then-active rail line. This community of individuals was the first and remains the most served group at Caminando Unidos.

The organization has shifted through the years from its start as a location made of corrugated steel for housing a small library that offered tutoring to the borrowing of a much larger space where rooms have been turned into small learning spaces and larger areas have been converted into arts and recreational zones. Caminando Unidos refers to themselves as an 'educational project', specifically not to be confused with a school so as not to imply the constraints and expectations (in their analysis, often brutalizing and dehumanizing, especially for the historically marginalized) (e.g. Prakash & Esteva, 1998). Through thoughtful and iterative analysis, the project organizers have followed its most recent evolution through the teachings of Don Miguel Ruiz's Four Agreements (1997) and Juan David Garcia's Transformative Curriculum (2005). In short, they have created a system of values which can work for any civilization such as 'The bigger one takes care of the smaller one', and 'The one who knows more teaches the one who knows less', alongside gratitude, hospitality, and care, among others. It is no exaggeration to say that despite the social hardships endured in the community (thanks, in the most part, to structural sources of oppression), the participants in the program learn, live, and embody the values espoused at Caminando Unidos. Over the last ten years, I (Kasun) have observed the project's continued evolution and enjoyed watching her students grow and learn from their exposure.

Caminando Unidos has had an outward-facing orientation for well over a decade in terms of receiving international visitors. Some visitors spend an entire year working on the project; others are shorter-term, such as a sequence of daily visits with the participants of Caminando Unidos over a week. Through this reciprocal experience, visitors learn a new model of how to educate—profoundly—without formally creating a school and despite existing entirely off of donations and volunteer labor. The exposure often forces visitors to wonder, 'If Caminando Unidos can do this with so few resources, what might I be capable of in my own community?' The directors of the project are selective about allowing workshop providers and volunteer access while maintaining an attitude of openness to what we can learn from one another. I remember specifically that after my mother died a violent death by suicide in 2016, my first landing for research was specifically to engage the work of Caminando Unidos. I was able to see that despite horrible violence nearby, individuals were capable of caring for each other profoundly in community despite seemingly impossible hardships. The care the members of Caminando Unidos extended to me that summer left a mark on me that has not diminished, and I have, each year, returned to work with them with my study abroad students with a confidence that my students, too, will gain from their exposure.

The program participants made four visits to Caminando Unidos. The first day, they shared breakfast at the large communal tables with the youth. The food is a traditional Mexican breakfast, scratch-cooked by a cook and volunteers. The youth help distribute the meals to the 80 or so individuals who eat together. It was nutritious (e.g. beans and eggs with fruit) and also well-seasoned. Each participant, including guests, took their plate to the outdoor communal wash area and cleaned it. Then, on the first day, the students toured the facility and learned in a roundtable format what the organization had accomplished. The speaker, Lucy, explained through an interpreter that the organization had shifted a great deal over the 20-plus years it had been serving the community and that they were living their core values as best they could. The university students were then assigned to subsequent workshops, which would include visiting the mindfulness group, the music group, the outdoor agriculture group, and also to recreational activities with the young people participating, including a nearly daily soccer match on a lovely green donated in the last five years as well as other community-building activities that were well scaffolded by the guides. The university students observed how the participants used tools such as mindfulness and gratitude to explore challenging community dynamics while also co-creating a safe space for such exploration.

Several students spent a great deal of time during the program reflecting on what their four days of work with Caminando Unidos meant to them in class discussions and in their written responses. Silvia also felt a socioeconomic connection with the students in Caminando Unidos but realized that her space was different than the one she encountered in Mexico:

> I grew up really poor and there was a period in my life in which the only meals I had in a day were the ones that were provided at school. I have lived hunger and I have lived poverty. My identity is situated differently in this because the poverty that I lived in the States is different than the poverty lived by the Indigenous here in Mexico. In this respect I move into a position in which I have to recognize that the cultural impact and the ancestral history that comes with being underprivileged and Indigenous goes much deeper and is more profound than the type of poverty I lived. Not to say that one is less bad or that I did not suffer, but it is a different type of poverty.

Silvia felt a link with the marginalized people in the community, although she understood that her circumstances were different growing up in the Global North. Silvia's feelings of being marginalized in the Global North had parallels to the marginalization of Indigenous people in the Global South while she also recognized the additional racial discrimination dimensions of being Indigenous in Mexico. Her reflection illustrated her empathy with the children at the school. Through the feelings they were experiencing within the context of Mexico, the Latinx students described their stance and understanding of the complex intersections between the sociopolitical and socioeconomics of the Global South and Global North.

Through our immersion in Caminando Unidos, the Latinx students witnessed the relational approach in the school as students took responsibility for each other. This responsibility for each other extended to teachers and volunteers. Silvia noticed:

> As a volunteer, I noticed that no one assumes that you do or don't know how to do a task, but they do ask if it is something you are comfortable doing. They also don't expect more of me than I am willing to give.

Silvia also provided examples of the way the students are responsible toward each other:

> The pre-values say that the bigger person should take care of the smaller person and that the more knowledgeable person should teach the less knowledgeable one. During breakfast, the older kids help bring plates and drinks to the younger kids so that they can eat breakfast. Then, everyone would pick up their plates and wash them in the sink. It was amazing to see this comradery between all of the students, staff, and volunteers.

The Latinx students internalized these Indigenous ideas in the ways they observed the relations between all who were present in the school. Lupe wrote, 'Everyone's smiles and compassion that they shared with the kids were genuine and we were all incredibly touched to be a part of this'. The interactions between the Latinx students and the students at the Indigenous alternative school were impacted by the culture created. Jimena described the connections she made at the school, 'Each one of us got attached to a child'. Lupe observed, 'I was able to see all of my classmates interact with these little kids and I could see through every interaction, everyone was changed in a positive way'.

In Caminando Unidos, the idea of openly expressing feelings is a part of the culture of the school. Jimena said, 'By creating an environment where they can express themselves freely it is demonstrating to them not to hold back or hide what you feel or what you want to say'. Beyond the students in the alternative school listening to each other, they also value what others are saying. Another Latinx student noted that the school director was instrumental in creating the environment where students were to value other students' words as much as their own. A curriculum which emphasized the Toltec agreement 'Be impeccable with your word' and valuing other people's words required honesty. Therefore, there is an expectation that all answers to questions were answered honestly. Another focus the director and teachers expected from the students was participation. Silvia wrote how 'participation is important because it adds to the individuals experience but that it also adds to everyone else's'. Ana noted how she became aware of the alternate ways of teaching that relies on community and relational curricula.

Within the homestays, language schools, and Indigenous alternative schools, the Latinx students sensed the feeling of community. They talked about how everyone shared whatever they had such as food, resources, knowledge, or time with each other. The convivencia (living together in harmony) within the community made others feel a sense of belonging. Most of the Latinx students expressed feeling a part of the community as they used terms like 'family' in their reflections and discussions.

Conviviality of Homestay Experience

The Latinx students made connections to their homestay families which positively impacted their experience in Mexico. A relationship was formed through the careful placement of study abroad students with their homestay families. Each of the students in the study abroad program was placed into a homestay experience by the administrators at CILAC Freire. Before our travels to Mexico, the language school staff sent each of the students an application form. The information they gathered from this application was used for the homestay placement and for the development of Spanish classes. The social context of the homestay experience was significant to the students.

According to the director, Mata, the collaboration between the host families and CILAC Freire is an extension of the student immersion program. In the study by Knight and Schmidt-Rinehart (2002), the homestay families indicated that they felt they were a part of the study abroad experience and their role went beyond 'providing a safe, warm, and supportive environment for students' (p. 198). Although the host families saw themselves as caretakers for the students, Knight and Schmidt-Rinehart concluded that students did not fully appreciate all the opportunities the host families had to offer. The findings in this study highlight the close connections several of the students formed with their homestay families. The connections that occurred between the host families and study abroad students were the fruits of the thoughtful considerations the director of CILAC Freire used to match host families and students.

A unique connection was revealed in the data between Silvia and her homestay mom, Teresa. During the interview, Teresa described the ways she connected her study abroad students with the people in the community and the culture in Mexico during a visit to Tepoztlán:

> I'm an active feminist activist so there are always activities going on, meetings, and I talk to them about all of these. When we went to Tepoztlán, we all got together and then we saw a friend who is a filmmaker, and she is the director of a program called Telemanita and they have interesting videos about women. Through activities we get involved.

The student Silvia wrote about what she experienced and felt during the excursion to Tepoztlán with Teresa:

> We got to meet some of [Teresa's] good friends! These women were so wonderful to be around. They are self-proclaimed feminists and definitely live the lives of activists. Collectively their efforts include work for the UN in Egypt, working for women's rights and in Italy, and being part of the LGBTQ movement in Mexico. I really connected with their work.

The activities Teresa planned for her study abroad students resonated with Silvia on a personal level. In another reflection, Silvia disclosed how this experience with Teresa had reframed her thinking about her own culture and heritage. She reflected:

> I always found it hard to relate to the Hispanic community due to my feminist views. This trip in particular though, has opened my eyes to a Mexican community I had no idea existed. I had never heard of Mexican feminists until this trip, and I had never witnessed another Mexican speak so openly about LGBTQ rights.

Silvia's connection with the local community and her own identity may not have occurred if she had been situated with a different host family, perhaps families that had not received significant training as CILAC Freire has provided throughout the years, multiple times a year. The significance of the connection of Silvia's homestay arrangement correlates with the finding by Kobayashi and Viswat (2015), which stated that a study abroad director needs to gain information about each student before placement to enhance compatibility.

Students Lupe and Ana shared a homestay, and they each expressed their love for their host moms. Lupe said:

> I can't even lie, I got emotional saying goodbye. Because there were hardly any language barriers, it made it easy for all of us to feel like a family. Staying with them helped me get used to being in a different country because they felt so much like my real family.

Ana wrote, 'I was amazed at how much my host family felt like family. It was hard to accept that a place I had been in for only a few days felt more welcoming than the place I had lived in for almost 21 years'. Ricardo and Carlos describe their feelings of care and hospitality with their homestay mom. Ricardo noted, 'I have been lucky enough to stay in Cuernavaca, Mexico with a wonderful host mother'. Carlos exclaimed, 'My host mom was amazing. I feel like I created a really good bond with [Bella] and her motherly skills did show with the way she treated us'. The feelings they felt toward their homestay mom, Bella, was mutual. In an interview with Bella, she said, 'I love the fact that they feel comfortable, happy, peaceful and I'm too; there's no problems because the coexistence is beautiful'.

Kobayashi and Viswat (2015) state that positive outcomes in homestays occur 'when participants devised ways to bridge psychological and cultural differences' (p.484). In this study, the Latinx students identified a connection with the local community through language, new knowledge about communities in Mexico, and heritage. The Latinx students' family heritage established a cultural commonality with the host families and may have contributed to the close connections and the feeling 'like family' these students discovered with the host families. In this study abroad program, the director of CILAC Freire explained that 'there are a series of activities and commitments that [homestay families] must attend at the school throughout the year'. Activities in the school included workshops in psychology, group integration, homophobia, and Paulo Freire. Participation is also expected in an annual excursion with all the school staff. The specific expectations of the host families to be part of a learning community are well received by the host families. These interactions build relationships between the teachers at CILAC Freire and the homestay families as they form their own community. Everyone in the study abroad program benefited from the connections between the school and families through communal meals at the Spanish language school and the feelings of conviviality.

Kubota (2016) indicates that sociopolitics and socioeconomics are embedded in a homestay through issues of race, gender, ethnicity, sexuality, and others. The relationships between the study abroad students and the host families are complex. Capitalism does play a part in the homestay program through the exchange of money. Several host families indicated this was a reason for initially being a host family, but each host family stated this was not the reason they continue in the program. One of the host 'moms', Margarita, said, 'A friendship emerges, that affection, that trust, so, I try to look at it this way. It is a job, yes, thank God, but there's something more important, the friendship'. The relationships developed between the students and hosts during the homestay complicates the dynamics of the unequal power structures.

We also recognized the depths of the relationships created by the Latinx students within the study abroad group where everyone continued to interact beyond the scheduled program and participate in activities together. The relationships developed within the group may have limited the amount of time the Latinx students connected with their host families. Eva and I (Marks) intentionally included our host mom in several of our activities outside of the scheduled learning experiences. On several occasions, we insisted that she join us for dinner with the group when we were in the city center. I am not sure if including our host mom in unplanned events was related to age because the undergraduate students did not include their host families in these experiences.

A study abroad director needs to consider the relationships and strong connections the in-country program director has with the local community such as the host families. Before students in the study abroad program travel, the host country program director needs to collect information about the students and carefully consider the compatibility of the students with host families. While in the host country, the faculty director should create one or more opportunities for the students to interact in a meaningful way with their host families. The interactions experienced by the study abroad students in a homestay experience contribute to their connections and feelings about the local community.

Through the lived experiences of the Latinx students (both planned and spontaneous) during the study abroad program, the students connected with the local community. After being in Mexico and interacting with the local community, Celia stated, 'at the end of the day the people are the ones dealing with the power of the government'. This statement was derived from talks she had with her host family and their public activism. My (Marks) interview with Celia's host mom revealed the host mom's passion and commitment to Indigenous rights. Before arriving in Mexico, the Latinx students had learned very little about Indigenous culture and people through the Eurocentric education they received in the United States, which had in large part erased Indigenous culture (Battiste, 2013; Grande, 2015; Lomawaima & McCarty, 2006). What they found in Mexico was a thriving, if not subjugated, Indigenous culture that persisted despite genocide and racism (Bonfil Batalla, 1987) through everyday embodiment, ritual, dance, and language.

Reciprocity

'We are, one and all, social beings living in relation to one another' (Cajete, 2000, p. 90). Through reciprocity, we had a responsibility in this relationship to respect and care for each other. As a participant in the study abroad program, we each had a purpose and something to share. Relationships and reciprocity developed between all participants and the faculty through the acts of sharing, contributing, and being present while being vulnerable without judgment.

There were deeply established relationships between the teachers at CILAC Freire and the homestay families, and during these two weeks, they had lovingly invited us into their classrooms, homes, and lives. Bella, along with the other homestay families, expressed deep gratitude and affection for Jorge (Mata's husband and partner in CILAC Friere school), 'Jorge was a great friend. He supported us, helped us. I love him so much no matter he isn't here anymore'. Everyone in the study abroad program benefited from the connections and reciprocity between the school faculty and homestay families.

The relationship between the host family and the study abroad students was evident in the feelings expressed by both. Vélez-Ibáñez (1988) maintains 'reciprocity represents an attempt to establish a social relationship on an enduring basis' (p. 142). Acknowledging differences, the host families and study abroad students did not view socioeconomic or cultural difference as a barrier to strong affective connections. Familial ties developed between the host families and study abroad students for the brief time they spent together.

As a homestay mom, Donna described the reciprocity of learning from each other and respect between her and the homestay students:

> I have learned something from all the people that I have received. I think that one of the most important values is respect; because if there's respect you're going to have everything; you're going to have peace, serenity, you're going to have good relations. And I think that is the principal value and also the mutual knowledge that we get everyday from each other.

Participant Lupe described the relationships developed while living and learning with the homestay families:

> They treated us like their own daughters. No matter what our group did that day, where we went, or what we learned, they were there at the end of the day for us to tell them all about it. Staying with them helped us get used to being in a different country because they felt so much like family.

Lupe understood the homestay family's act of compassion by sharing their lives with the study abroad students. Through reciprocity, Lupe shared her own lived experiences. The emotions felt by the participating students and the homestay families illustrated their mutual care toward each other.

Ana had similar feelings about her homestay experience, 'I was amazed at how much my host family felt like family. Like an aunt and grandma, I was visiting'. Carlos also had a connection to his host mom, 'I created a really good bond with [host mom] and I would love to visit her again'. The homestay opportunity allowed the Latinx students to form relationships within the community. These relationships went beyond casual acquaintance for the moment of time the Latinx students and homestay families became family. The host mom, Margarita, shared her feelings about the study abroad participants which mirrors the feelings the students expressed:

> To me it has been a joy to have the students at home and I'll tell you again that I'm a crying baby and sometimes I need to hold my tears when they leave; when they leave, I feel like a family member left, not a student. To me the word student doesn't exist. When they come to my door with their luggage I tell them; come in, this is your house.

During this study abroad program, there was mutual respect and care between the homestay families, teachers at CILAC Freire, and students at Caminando Unidos.

Within our study abroad group, all participants shared personal stories and opened themselves to others in the group. Carlos described the connection and feelings of reciprocity within the group, 'I will always remember the bond that we created as a group. We shared some personal stories that we wouldn't just share with anyone. Everyone was meant to be on this program together'. Eva explained this connection, 'I feel happy to have allowed myself to feel vulnerable, to laugh, and cry with no fear and shame. I was able to open my heart, receive hugs, care, and friendships with no limits'. Ricardo described his experience during the program, 'I really liked how our class came together as a family. We were open and accepting of one another'. The Latinx students felt solidarity within the study abroad group as everyone experienced classes, the immersion school experience, and activities together.

The study abroad program was designed for everyone to have their own personal encounter, build community within the group, and at the end of the experience be able to connect more effectively with people in the local community of Cuernavaca. Through this study abroad program, we were able to reconnect with feminist and Indigenous knowledges that would help us survive and thrive communally with love.

References

Anzaldúa, G. (2002). Now let us shift...the path of conocimiento...inner work, public acts. In G. Anzaldúa & A. L. Keating (Ed.), *This bridge we call home* (pp. 540–578). New York: Routledge.

Battiste, M. (2013). *Decolonizing education: Nourishing the learning spirit*. Vancouver, BC: Purich Publishing.

Bonfil Batalla, G. (1987). *México Profundo: Una Civilización Negada*, Mexico: Editorial *Grijalba*.

Brown, B. (2008). *I thought it was just me (but it isn't): Making the journey from "What will people think" to "I am enough"*. New York: Avery.

Cajete, G. (2000). *Native science: Natural laws of interdependence*. Sante Fe, NM: Clear Light Pub.

Freire, P. (2000). *Pedagogy of the oppressed*. New York: Bloomsbury Academic.

Garcia, J. D. (2005). *Creative transformation: A practical guide for maximizing creativity*. (n.p.): Whitmore Publishing Company.

Grande, S. (2015). *Red pedagogy: Native American social and political thought* (10th ed.). Lanham, Maryland: Rowman & Littlefield.

Hartman, E., Reynolds, N. P., Ferrarini, C., Messmore, N., Evans, S., Al-Ebrahim, B., & Brown, J. M. (2020). Coloniality-decoloniality and critical global citizenship: Identity, belonging and education abroad. *Frontiers: The Interdisciplinary Journal of Study Abroad, XXXII*(2), 33–59.

Knight, S., & Schmidt-Rinehart, B. (2002). Enhancing the homestay: Study abroad from the host family's perspective. *Foreign Language Annals, 35*(2), 190–201.

Kobayashi, J., & Viswat, L. (2015). A relational approach to international education through homestay programs. *Journal of International Student, 5*(4), 475–487.

Kubota, R. (2016). The social imaginary of study abroad: Complexities and contradictions. *The Language Learning Journal, 44*(3), 347–357.

Lomawaima, K. T., & McCarty, T. L. (2006). *"To remain an Indian": Lessons in democracy from a century of Native American education*. Teachers College Press.

Mohanty, C. T. (2003). *Feminism without borders: Decolonizing theory, practicing solidarity*. Durham, NC: Duke University Press.

Peat, D. (2002). *Blackfoot physics: A journey into the Native American universe*. Boston: Weiser Books.

Pirbhai Illich, F., & Martin, F. (2019). Decolonizing teacher education in immersion contexts: Working with space, place, and boundaries. In D. Martin & E. Smolcic (Eds.), *Redefining teaching competence through immersive programs:*

Practices for culturally sustaining classrooms (pp. 65–93). London: Palgrave Macmillan. https://doi.org/10.1007/978-3-030-24788-1

Prakash, M., & Esteva, G. (1998). *Escaping education: Living as learning within grass-roots cultures* (Counterpoints; Vol. 36 ed.). New York: Peter Lang.

Ruiz, D. M. (1997). *The four agreements: A Toltec wisdom book*. San Rafael, CA: Amber-Allen.

Vélez-Ibáñez, C. (1988). Networks of exchange among Mexicans in the U.S. and Mexico: Local level mediating responses to national and international transformation. *Urban Anthropology, 17*. 27–51.

5 How International Study Creates Opportunities for Personal/Communal Solidarity through Continued Mother Tongue Maintenance, Political Consciousness, and Identity

The students struggled and confronted the impact of colonization on their education and the socioeconomics of the Global North and Global South. They realized the fragmentation of their languages and identities caused by colonization. The study abroad program was a decolonizing experience which provided an opportunity for the students to feel whole and to examine the ways they could enact change against oppressive structures.

As explored in the introduction, we recognize how hegemonic U.S. culture readily rebuffs non-dominant challenges to Whiteness. One of the strongest possibilities for identic survival is thus a reprieve from the domination of the United States culturally while immersing oneself in an(O)ther context. The flipping of frames and scripts in terms of race and language in the international program context thus provides new spaces of possibility, consideration, deep reflection toward (re)engaging one's identity, language skill sets, and political consciousness.

In this chapter, student experiences are explored as evidence of feeling newly included in community, linguistically and racially. The Latinx students reconnected with their own internal selves in ways that empowered them and transformed their feelings of cultural marginalization with the ability to carry forward a personal identity toolkit upon return to the hostile U.S. terrain where Whiteness slips into the majoritarian norm for being.

Indeed, when we landed in Mexico City to start our program, students were already speaking Spanish in the airport as they connected their fluency in Spanish with their Latin American heritage. Some of this we attribute to the work we did prior to departure with the students to claim their heritages to sense-make their own language journeys during their lives and how we encouraged them to feel comfortable with all their language uses. We only set the stage, however. When the students spoke with each other, they bonded over their adaptive strategies in speaking Spanish and English and formed solidarity by being comfortable with their mix of languages. They gained agency by feeling content to speak and be

DOI: 10.4324/9781003320111-6

multilingual and include words and terms that encapsulate Spanish and English. Students expressed how being and interconnecting within heritage spaces in Mexico made them confront and disrupt their own thinking about themselves toward a new way of interconnecting with people and places.

Consciousness of Alternative Understandings of Language

Languages are a social construct with assumptions about purity and fixity (e.g. Pennycook & Makoni, 2020). That is to say, those with the power to do so have named and claimed certain language practices as *official, correct*, and following the *rules* of grammar and syntax. As such, the custodians of 'proper' usage of the language then have the power to label and literally exclude forms of language usage. Throughout human history, however, language was used for the purpose of communication to greater and lesser extents without these excluding taxonomies. Linguistics has deep roots in colonization, which means that language has been defined and analyzed through Western thought and letters. As such, language has then become a tool of power if not also deep forms of oppression. One of the easiest examples is how bilingual Spanish and English speakers have been told that their 'Spanglish' is somehow inappropriate often from monolingual English speakers! This colonizing construct leads to the nationalization of languages, or the association of one (or more) languages being often officially designated as the language(s) of the nation state or being understood as such. The efforts of this program were to challenge these colonizing assumptions toward embracing greater hybrid uses of language while stitching these reclamations into identity while also acknowledging that language and identity would play out differently in the Mexican context.

From the minute we stepped off the plane into Mexico, we noticed how the Latinx students were eager and ready to speak Spanish, more so than while they lived in the United States. They spoke to each other in Spanish, and our CILAC Freire guide spoke only Spanish as we explored Mexico City. Once in Cuernavaca, the teachers at CILAC Freire, guest speakers, and homestay families spoke to us almost exclusively in Spanish, as was their practice and the objective of their wanting to share their cultural language with us. On one of our first nights in Cuernavaca, we all gathered together at a restaurant in the center of the city and sat at a table together. Everyone was speaking Spanish, which we knew was one of the wonderful ways the students were connecting to the country and feeling a part of the community.

The ability to connect within Mexico was in contrast to many of the students' experiences within the United States. Carlos expressed his frustration when he was immersed in a different language and culture after moving from the Dominican Republic to the United States: 'I had to learn a whole new language while also being expected to thrive in school simultaneously so that I would not get too far behind. I remember how much hard work and time I spent in order to master the language and culture'. He did not give up his knowledge of Spanish or culture from the Dominican Republic while living in the Global North and further understanding the dominant language, English. The Latinx students connected their fluency in the Spanish language with their Latin American heritage and the local community in Mexico.

While in Mexico, the students were confronted with images and interactions indicating colorism and assumptions about language. Colonization of Latin America permeates with a hierarchy of race with colorism embedded in all parts of Mexican society (Alim et al., 2016; Mignolo, 2011a; Quijano, 2000). Two of the Latinx students were confronted by local people with false beliefs about their Latin American heritage correlating with their Spanish fluency. Oscar and Carlos described how people in Mexico made assumptions based on the function of their phenotype about their abilities to speak and understand the language (Alim et al., 2016). These assumptions appear to be based on colorism, which we explore below.

Oscar, being fair skinned and whose heritage is based in Spain and Puerto Rico, described two encounters that led him to realize that people in Mexico often did not see him as Latin American. He wrote:

> Many of the people here in Mexico that I've met over the past four days automatically assume that it is unlikely that I can speak Spanish. The shaman at the zocalo in la Cuidad de Mexico, for example, felt the need to ask me if I spoke Spanish, as did my host parents.

Carlos was an Afrolatino from the Dominican Republic whose multilingual proficiency surprised individuals in Mexico who did not expect him to speak Spanish. Carlos explains, 'I have had Latino people in various schools argue with me and tell me that I am not Dominican due to the fact that I have a darker skin. They would tell me that I am just a black person that happens to know Spanish but that I am not Latino'. As in the United States, a phenotype-based identity is applied to Carlos, marginalizing his identity based on language and ethnicity. Assumptions by people in Mexico about others' ability to speak and understand the language was not unique to Mexico. In the United States, people also hold beliefs about the Latinx students and their use of language by suggesting they replace Spanish with English, as if this would somehow give them a greater advantage to adapt to the United States while all the while the research indicates that multilingualism is always of greater benefit for the speaker. Students knowing more than one language develop complex skills by reorganizing thoughts and creating connections among different symbols (Ben-Zeev, 1977; Bialystok, 1991). Knowing more than one language is always an asset.

Realizing that neither Latinx people are a monolith nor is their language, the Latinx students listened to the stories and lived experiences from local activists who advocated for people throughout Latin America. Oscar became cognizant of his belief that all people in Latin America spoke Spanish; then, he understood this assumption was wrong as he listened to a testimonial during a language class:

> I just thought it was crazy how people who fled Guatemala to go to Mexico, some of them couldn't even speak Spanish. Because when you think about it, Guatemala's like, 'Oh yeah, it's a Spanish-speaking country.' But there's so many communities where Spanish isn't the first language, which I think is fascinating.

He, like the other students, realized the plurality of languages within a country and the significance of Indigenous languages to their identity and community, which was one of several decolonial aims of the overall program. The guest speaker was an activist Maya Guatemalan shaman who had fled civil war in the 1980s of Guatemala.

The Latinx students sometimes struggled to navigate 'formal' Spanish (we recognize formal gets to be claimed by those with the power to code and sort it) while in Mexico versus their ability to speak Spanish in the United States. In the United States, their Spanish was considered fluent, although in Mexico their Spanish was considered flawed as they mixed Spanish with words associated with Chicanx communities. Lupe described her frustration with perceptions about her Spanish language abilities:

> This Spanish class was honestly one of the hardest things about this study abroad. Not hard in terms of it was hard learning grammar, it was just hard to be told that your way of speaking is wrong. It was hard going through a small identity crisis so early in the morning, but I discovered that this experience reassured me of my Xicana identity.

While Lupe understood this as being told that her Spanish was 'wrong', we recognize the teachers of CILAC Freire work with Chicanx, Latinx, and many pan-Latinx people frequently toward the goal of sharing the general forms of usage of Spanish as they live it in Mexico. Indeed, we have discussed with the teachers our concerns that engaging the instruction of Spanish and culture (as the classes at CILAC Freire are heavily embedded in cultural transmission and sharing) not be a further colonizing experience. That said, students often are shocked that the codes they engage of Spanish and Spanglish in the United States do not fully mesh with those of Mexican Spanish.

Jimena wrote about the disconnect between her fluency in Spanish in the United States compared to how she felt about her fluency in Mexico:

> In the United States, I considered myself fluent in Spanish because I could understand what was being said to me and I could form a response. I also utilized words that are non-existent in Latin American countries. Chequear, taggear, yarda, Maarqueta, are words that Latinos living in the United States created. However, I have found myself getting choked up when I am speaking either in class or outside the classroom setting.

The benefits of linguistic gains are a focus within the body of literature on study abroad programs (Guerrero, 2006; Kubota, 2016; Smolcic & Katunich, 2017). Linguistic competence is problematized by the assumption that 'language learning tends to be based on standard language ideology, contradicting the recent dynamic view of language arising from the globalization trend of linguistic practices that challenge the traditional notion of language as a bounded and fixed entity' (Kubota, 2016, p. 352). The Latinx students experienced the conflicting feelings of lacking competence in formal Spanish in Mexico, although they felt comfortable with their Spanish in the United States.

In the course readings, Gloria Anzaldúa (1987) wrote about being uncomfortable speaking Spanish in front of Latinas because she was afraid of their censure. She then goes on to mention that she often found herself, along with other Spanish speakers, speaking English at parties and conferences, but also being afraid of appearing too *agringada* to them. One of the students, Silvia, connected her lived experience to the course readings by Anzaldúa. Her self-criticism of her abilities in Spanish spilled over into her own identity.

> My academic world consists of solely speaking English and hardly ever speaking Spanish, if at all. When I am confronted with a room of other Latinx colleagues I find myself often trying really hard to exude my Latinx-ness. It is a weird dichotomy because it only happens to me when other Latinx folk are around. I don't ever exude that kind of pride or cultural characterization with non-Hispanic colleagues in my world.

The students realized they were in a liminal space with their understanding of English and Spanish and wanted their new function of language to be recognized. Carlos stated, 'I have decided to not be afraid to use my right of speaking Spanish freely'. Ricardo also expressed his thoughts about freely speaking Spanish in the United States:

> There have been numerous occasions in which I was othered for speaking Spanish in public with family and friends in the United States. I actively make sure to not allow anyone to make anyone else or myself feel inferior for speaking a certain language.

These statements reflect the connection between identity and language and the impact on a person's sense of self (Alim et al., 2016).

There was also, at times, resistance by the Latinx students to the Spanish language instruction in the language school in Mexico. Lupe described her heritage as it pertains to language in the United States and her feelings about her heritage language in Mexico, while critiquing the formalization of the Spanish language:

> I never received the formal Spanish language education. This Spanish education comes straight from the people I communicate with and how we have developed our own language in a way. All of this to ask, how strictly should I be criticized by Mexican people who have only ever spoken in native Spanish speaking dialect about my Spanish that I have accumulated existing in a different country? Languages are constantly changing, who is there to say that I am correct to say 'parkear' in my own regard. In my culture as a Xicana, those Spanglish terms are not only common, but correct. There is an understanding, however, that I am here to learn this 'correct' Spanish. It is not ideal to be told that my identity as a Xicana and the cultural and language differences that come with it is wrong. It is simply just different than Mexican culture and their interpretation of the Spanish language.

Language was expressed as part of the Latinx students' identity as they resisted any efforts to conform to only speaking English or formal Spanish furthering their own identity and sense of self. The notion of expertise in a language was problematized by the Latinx students while in Mexico. They resisted a Global North conception that languages are fixed (Pennycook & Makoni, 2020). Living in the Global North with cultural connections to the Global South, the Latinx students bonded over their adaptive strategies toward language and, therefore, decolonized their use of language.

Developing and Enhancing a Political Consciousness

We had been unable to visit the Museum of Indomitable Memory, a museum that explores the struggles and victories of those who fight for the recovery of the more than 100,000 disappeared Mexicans by the government and other entities, because our planned visit coincided with Mother's Day in Mexico, and the museum decided to close and honor mothers. The museum experience in the past had been an early part of the program to contextualize that many of Mexico's folkloric stories are like all nation state's stories—myths that often cover more vexing histories. The museum also expertly links corruption to authorities and the powerful with the United States so that participants are disabused of the idea that corruption is somehow innate only to Mexico.

Martha, the CILAC Freire director, made sure we discussed some of these issues and struggles in front of the Morelos State Government Palace in the heart of downtown Cuernavaca two days later during our tour of the city. The large, colonial-looking edifice had iron gates at the front that were nearly always locked, yet in protest loved ones were allowed to leave images and plaques about the deceased and the disappeared. Faces from as far back as 30 years ago were etched in the memories of their loved ones and in hard-backed, color, and black-and-white photo plaques with names written underneath, often with no year for a death, only a year listed for a birth, Martha explained. The students grew intensely quiet and focused as she explained what the images of 100 or more people were about. 'Others are now officially gone, such as famed activist Samir Flores who was just assassinated a month ago for trying to protect the lands from a nuclear power plant that no one other than the government and the rich want'. Students asked if there was any way to protect these kinds of activists. Martha, after her decades of *lucha* in Mexico said, only the valiant do the work and that we all need to have the *valentia* to do so.

Rewriting their personal knowledge of the history in Mexico during the study abroad program transformed the way the Latinx students understood history and themselves. Unsettling the Eurocentric way of thinking of the dominant culture in the United States, the Latinx students took a decolonized stance as they learned a more pluralistic view of the world (Battiste, 2013; Grande, 2015; Walsh, 2007). The Latinx students were free to produce their own knowledge as they juxtaposed the Western discourse they learned in the Global North with their experiential learning in the study abroad program, as they visited historical places, listened to testimonials, and became aware of alternative views.

Grande (2015) explains that the project of decolonization is a collaboration between the teacher and students to change the history presented to them by people in the West. We gained awareness about problems on either side of the border in Mexico through the critical readings on neoliberalism and colonization (Bigelow, 2006; Mignolo, 2011b) and study abroad (Chang, 2017; Illich, 1968). We learned by engaging in meaningful and intentional class discussions with the faculty director and in the social justice-oriented classes at CILAC Freire interweaving local cultural issues into the curriculum.

One of the curricular moments created by the Spanish language school was a charla/testimonial by local activists who support the Indigenous and Zapatista movement in Chiapas, Mexico. The Zapatista cause is a local vision and not a global movement for all marginalized people. Their decolonized vision is encapsulated in the statement 'a world in which many worlds coexist' (un mundo en el que co-existan muchos mundos) (Mignolo, 2011a, p. 273). The Zapatistas emphasize dignity, belonging, and collective ownership which is expressed in the motto 'Para Todos Todo, Para Nosotros Nada *Everything for Everyone, Nothing for Us*' (Esteva, 2005, p. 130). The resistance movement of the Zapatistas occurred in south Mexico in 1994 at the moment the North American Free Trade Agreement (NAFTA) was implemented (Bigelow, 2006). The NAFTA trade agreement closely linked the economies of the United States and Mexico through its neoliberal agenda, which took advantage of cheap labor and land in Mexico. Within the topics of the course, the students learned, and one student stated, 'the economic fate of Mexico is tied to that of the United States through things like NAFTA'. While the Zapatista rebellion appeared as a reaction to NAFTA, the indigenous communities have lived with 500 years of colonial oppression comprised of privatizations and forfeiture of their land.

The invited charla of two activist guest speakers about the Zapatista movement gave Ana a new insight into the history of resistance by Indigenous people in Mexico. She made a connection between her own personal history and the Zapatistas, who were enacting change for Indigenous and other marginalized populations:

> The people that spoke at this charla had family that were involved or impacted by [Zapatista] movements, they come from a long heritage of revolutionaries. When I was 10 and marched in DC for an immigration reform, or when I was 15 marching in front of the state capital, I saw the same fire burning as I did this week in the Zapatistas. I obviously didn't know it then but the Mexican people's journey through history has crafted a way of knowing that shapes them into naturally born revolutionaries. This way of knowing teaches you not to give up 'si se puede' and your fight even if it means losing your life because that's how worth it the cause is. Of course, this doesn't apply to everyone, but it certainly applied to the people at the charla that day and the people I saw march on Washington when I was ten.

Along with Ana, Lupe also realized the impact of unjust systems within Mexico as she felt Mexican institutions negatively impacted Indigenous people and communities who live in poverty. Raising consciousness about unjust global realities, a person gains knowledge of differences as they relate to the contexts in which different cultures developed and with 'an understanding that there are as many differences within cultures as there are between them' (Pirbhai-Illich & Martin, 2019, p. 75). Lupe wrote, 'Mexico and the United States share this mistreatment of their lower-class communities'. Jimena noted the problems on both sides of the border as she reflected, 'In Mexico, immigrants from Central America are not taken in a welcoming manner in contrast to citizens of other countries. The prejudice and ignorance are evident in both cases [the United States and Mexico]'. As participants in the study abroad program, we were conscious of the significance of colonization on both sides of the border as it divided and oppressed people who were not White Europeans. The continuation of colonizing ideology was evident in both the United States and Mexico as the Latinx students described the injustice experienced by marginalized people.

Oscar immersed himself in the subjugated history of Mexico that seemed nonexistent in education in the Global North but presented itself in physical ways while in Mexico:

> The residue of colonialist and imperialist ideology, the specter of social Darwinism, paints other forms of knowledge that aren't *official* as being less important and often invalid. One of the things that struck me most was how there were so many instances of violent repression of speech on the part of the government. I had never before heard of the protests and subsequent violent repressions of Mactumactza and other such rural schools, nor had I been aware of the disappearance of 43 students from Ayotzinapa who were protesting the government's actions. What I learned on this trip about these campaigns of terror, and of the revolutionary resistance to them, is a concept that I will keep in mind the rest of my life.

Ana and Oscar listened to the testimonials and changed their ideas about revolutionaries being in the past by acknowledging the current circumstances of the lived experiences of people in Mexico. They both mention how their consciousness had been raised by learning about these revolutionaries in Mexico.

Silvia gained a new perspective on the people in Mexico while disrupting what she knew from her own family and her education in the United States. She wrote:

> This trip in particular though, has opened my eyes to the amount of progress the Mexican community has undergone or has opened my eyes to a Mexican community I had no idea existed. I had never heard of Mexican feminists until this trip, and I had also never witnessed another Mexican speak so openly about LGBTQ rights.

She began to question norms and expectations many young Latinx encounter in their families in the Global North. Silvia disrupted images and views of family expectations in the United States and gained a new perspective and feeling of solidarity with the Latina feminists she encountered during the study abroad program.

According to Grande (2015), the knowledge in Western schools is based on the hegemonic worldview situated in Eurocentric discourse. The new knowledge gained during the experiential study abroad program provided other perspectives about Latin America for the Latinx students. They gained a realistic and critical view of the country. Jimena described her relearning of history and moving forward to not let others determine the way history is conveyed in the Global North:

> Coming here and having the opportunity to learn not just about my culture but about the rich history and the problems it faces today. I have learned that it is important to be informed but even more important to be part of the change you want to see.

Ricardo adjusted his knowledge of the people and place as he said, 'When I can see all of the sides, the bigger picture is formed and I can work toward progress and improvement'. Ricardo knows the education he received in the United States is presented with one perspective and lacks critical frames of reference. Ana, Lupe, Jimena, Ricardo, and Oscar expressed wanting to be catalysts for change as they experienced and listened to the local community, while making connections to their own lives.

Common Connections through Identity

Ana, Carlos, Jimena, Ricardo, Lupe, and Silvia all shared their image about themselves in the Global North and their feelings of connection to the culture and people in Mexico while acknowledging differences. The Latinx students' connection to people and place made them feel at home as they internalized their family stories and culture, which tethered them to Latin America. Ana grappled with her own identity as Mexican American within the dominant culture in the United States as she wrote, 'There was a time when I tried hard to negate my Mexican heritage in effort to assimilate better into the mainstream culture, but at some point, I realized that I was tired of trying to fit in other people's boxes'. Silvia was another Latinx who often reflected about being marginalized by the dominant culture in the United States, while Carlos expressed a feeling of 'living in a country that is not my own' when he talked about the United States. In her first thoughts about being in Mexico, Jimena stated, 'I was finally in the country I had wanted to visit my whole life. The country where my parents are from and the country that holds all of my background histories'. Then, Jimena felt a sense of disorientation within the culture she encountered in Mexico:

> Another culture difference I encountered was in the food. Coming to Mexico, I thought that I was going to know all about the food and be able to tell them, 'yeah I know what that is-I eat that all the time.' I was embarrassed to ask what a certain dish was on the menu ...I felt like I should know since I was a so-called Mexican.

She was certain when she arrived in Mexico that food would be a very familiar part of the culture that she grew up with in the United States but was surprised when she realized the disconnect between knowing a culture within the Global North and experiencing the actual local culture. The immersion of an education abroad program afforded Jimena and the other Latinx students to reflect and gain a new perspective through this experiential learning experience.

Through family stories and heritage, the Latinx students had an intertwined connection to the history and culture in Latin America and their own identity. These students expanded or changed their feelings about their identity within the spaces of the United States, Mexico, and other Latin American countries. Even though Ricardo was from Colombia, he felt a connection to the culture in Mexico. Ricardo wrote:

> In retrospect, Mexico feels familiar to me. I do not feel like I am somewhere completely unknown that I do not belong in. The similar feeling that Mexico gives me that reminds me of Colombia helps me feel more at ease and at home here.

While talking in one of our classes, one student described the feeling of many of the Latinx students about returning to the United States: 'Back to being American'. This statement reflected the feelings of loss of identity by the Latinx students. The Latinx student recognized a separateness to being American in Mexico that is different than their identity in the United States. While in Mexico, Oscar shifted his expanding ideas about his own identity mix of European and Latin American, 'I recently found myself identifying as more Boricua than American or Spanish. I do think, however, that my identity is also expanding in the sense that I am getting a better grasp of what it means to be Hispanic and Latino'. Being in Mexico, Oscar learned more about his Latin heritage versus his European heritage from Spain and was impacted by his sense of pride in being Latinx. Ricardo plainly stated his feelings about how society has interacted with him as Latinx and the new space he created for his own identity:

> This is my first time in Mexico, and since I spend all of my life in the United States, my self-identity is slightly different in the two countries. In the United States, I typically identify as mainly Latino, multicultural, and transnational, with an emphasis on my latinidad. Here in Mexico, I am ultimately viewed as an American above anything... Due to my strong identification and pride in my latinidad, I stopped caring whether others accepted or how they viewed me, because at the end of the day I knew that no one could take who I am or the culture I am a part of away from me. Since arriving in Mexico, my identity has shifted, or expanded, without actually realizing it.

Ricardo, Oscar, and Lupe perceived their commonalities with the local Latin American community, while also noticing the differences. Keating (2013) stated, 'Commonalities are complex points of connection that both incorporate and move beyond sameness, similarity, and difference; commonalities acknowledge and include difference' (p. 42). Lupe felt disconnected to her community in the United States and the Mexican culture she encountered as she expressed feeling 'foreign' everywhere she went. She reconciled her feelings of an ambiguous identity by accepting her multiple intersectionalities:

> When it came to the environment in school, additionally, it was impossible to fit in with the middle-class American gifted students who have always known their path. I was low-income, first generation, and Mexican, in fact, the only one that was in the gifted classes. I had to constantly put up with comments about how I was going to end up pregnant at 16 like most Mexican women, and how I was never going to be smart enough because I was Mexican. I could only fit in with them when it came to the classes, but I did not have anything else in common in terms of culture or in terms of socio-economic status. I was barely fitting in with my own Latino community as it was, now I had to struggle with finding my place in American society as well. It is a disheartening feeling as though I could not fit in with my Mexican community nor my American community in school. I was too 'American' and 'smart' for the Mexicans, but too 'dumb' and 'Mexican' for the Americans...I am blessed with the radiant culture of my parent's ancestry and the modern culture that I have accumulated myself.
>
> Up until high school, I identified as Mexican. I knew, however, that I was not like the Mexicans who lived in Mexico. No matter how Mexican my parents were, I simply did not have the same culture or upbringing that I would have if I did live in Mexico. Eventually in high school, I discovered that there was a name for the identity that I've always struggled with. Xicana was the name of this group of people, my group of people, and I felt like I was introduced into a completely new world of identities and even cultures.

Here in Mexico, my identity as a Xicana is heightened. Again, I always knew that I wasn't just Mexican and that my culture and upbringing would be different than that of Mexicans who were born in Mexico.

In course readings and class discussions, the Latinx students learned more about themselves as transnationals and how often transnationals feel that they do not belong to the dominant culture or the culture of their family as they live in two different worlds (Kasun & Saavedra, 2014; Suárez-Orozco et al., 2015). Jimena felt friends and family defined her differently than how she identified herself. The statement she made about her space of identity was a common expression 'Ni de aqui ni de alla', which means, neither from here nor there. This statement is a deficit way of thinking about yourself and a feeling you do not belong in any place. Transnational is a multiplicity of identities and represents the opposite of *ni de aqui ni de alla*. We discussed in class the opportunity of being and belonging to both places, which creates a liminal space for new possibilities. During her reflections, Jimena reconciled her spaces of being:

> I identify myself as Mexican American. However, in the eyes of my peers, I am identified as just Mexican and in the eyes of my family, I am identified as just American. I cannot be both in their eyes because I am not American enough nor Mexican enough. 'Ni de aqui ni de alla'. How can I claim to be Mexican when I speak different Spanish than people from Mexico? I feel like in order to be happy with who I am and what I am, I have to accept my flaws to better myself. I have to stop and admit to myself that my Spanish has gotten weaker, by admitting it, it does not mean that I am any less Hispanic, Latina, Mexican, Mexican-American or whatever I am.

Silvia described a situated identity where her identity is fluid in different spaces (Keating, 2013):

> My identity is situated differently here because of many different factors. For one, back in the States I am Latina, Mexican, or Hispanic. I am not typically considered American by my peers or other Americans. When people ask me for my background, I typically say that I was born in California and the question that follows is typically one that asks for a clarification of my ethnic origin. Here in Mexico though, I am not necessarily Mexican. I am American or a *guerita*. These questions or statements typically don't offend me, but they do make me question my place in society.

The fluidity of identity was also a part of Eva's lived experience as she moved from Colombia to the United States and then to Mexico with her husband and children. Her journey as a graduate student needed to be completed in Mexico. She wrote about the shifting feelings of being in the United States and the feelings of being at home within the community in Mexico:

> We moved here in January, after living in the U.S. for 20 years. So going back to what you said, we feel safer here. And we constantly talk to my husband because he, at work for example, we keep talking that he feels like himself. Like he went back to what he was when we were living in Colombia, instead of the person that we were supposed to be while we were working in the U.S.

Eva and her family clearly felt a sense of safety in expressing their culture and heritage while openly being themselves in Latin America that they did not feel in the United States.

Celia justified her liminal feelings of identity in different places in the following reflection:

> During my visit to Mexico, I also learned more about my identity. I finally understood that I am an exquisite linguistic and cultural mix. I learned to see my life and experiences as part of a rich and diverse limbo, and to stop thinking that I don't belong anywhere.

The Latinx students understood and lived intersectionality through their recognition that multiple social divisions exist beyond a singular axis of race, ethnicity, gender, class, or language (Hill Collins & Bilge, 2016). Being in the United States and Mexico, they experienced different feelings about their identity through intersectionality. The feelings of marginality within the United States were noted in the Latinx students' reflections. The Latinx students acknowledged a commonality among themselves with having Latin American heritage and living in the Global North. This connection between the Latinx students is expressed by Ana in her reflection, 'There is a certain comradery that comes along with being Mexican or Hispanic. This comradery brings people together and feeds a sense of pride and belonging'.

Throughout the study abroad program, the Latinx students began to separate from the historical, ideological, and institutional powers that oppress and the hierarchal thinking which marginalizes them through Eurocentric discourses. They struggled and confronted the impact of colonization on their education and the socioeconomics of the Global North and the Global South. They realized the fragmentation of their languages and identities caused by colonization. The study abroad program was a decolonizing experience which provided an opportunity for the students to feel whole and to examine the ways they could enact change against oppressive structures.

References

Alim, H. S., Rickford, J., & Ball, A. (Eds.). (2016). *Raciolinguistics: How language shapes our ideas about race*. New York: Oxford University Press.

Anzaldúa, G. (1987). *How to tame a wild tongue. Borderlands: The new mestiza- la frontera* (pp. 75–86). San Francisco: Aunt Lute Book Company.

Battiste, M. (2013). *Decolonizing education: Nourishing the learning spirit*. Vancouver, BC: Purich Publishing.

Ben-Zeev, S. (1977). The influence of bilingualism on cognitive strategy and cognitive development. *Child Development, 48*, 1009–1018.

Bialystok, E. (1991). *Language processing in bilingual children*. New York, NY: Cambridge University Press.

Bigelow, B. (2006). NAFTA and the roots of migration. In *The line between us: Teaching about the border and Mexican immigration* (pp. 19–27). Milwaukee, WI: Rethinking Schools, Ltd.

Chang, A. (2017). 'Call me a little critical if you will': Counterstories of Latinas studying abroad in Guatemala. *Journal of Hispanic Higher Education, 16*(1), 3–23.

Esteva, G. (2005). Celebration of Zapatismo. *Humboldt Journal of Social Relations, 29*(1), 127–167.

Grande, S. (2015). *Red pedagogy: Native American social and political thought* (10th ed.). Lanham, Maryland: Rowman & Littlefield.

Guerrero, E., Jr. (2006). *The road less traveled: Latino students and the impact of studying abroad*. (Unpublished Doctoral Dissertation). University of California Los Angeles, Retrieved from Dissertation Abstracts International. (AAT 3249418).

Hill Collins, P., & Bilge, S. (2016). *Intersectionality*. Malden, MA: Polity Press.

Illich, I. (1968). To hell with good intentions. Paper presented at the *Conference on InterAmerican Student Projects (CIASP)*, Cuernavaca, Mexico.

Kasun, G. S., & Saavedra, C. M. (2014). Crossing borders towards young transnational lives. In J. Keengwe & G. Onchwari (Eds.) *Cross-cultural considerations in the education of young immigrant learners* (pp. 200–216). Hershey, PA: IGI Global.

Keating, A. (2013). *Transformation now! toward a post-oppositional politics of change*. Urbana, IL: University of Illinois Press.

Kubota, R. (2016). The social imaginary of study abroad: Complexities and contradictions. *The Language Learning Journal, 44*(3), 347–357.

Mignolo, W. (2011a). *The darker side of western modernity: Global futures, decolonial options*. Durham, NC: Duke University Press.

Mignolo, W. (2011b). Geopolitics of sensing and knowing: On (de)coloniality, border thinking and epistemic disobedience. *Postcolonial Studies, 14*(3), 273–283.

Pennycook, A., & Makoni, S. (Eds.). (2020). *Innovations and challenges in applied linguistics from the Global South*. London: Routledge.

Pirbhai-Illich, F., & Martin, F. (2019). Decolonizing teacher education in immersion contexts: Working with space, place, and boundaries. In D. Martin & E. Smolcic (Eds.), *Redefining teaching competence through immersive programs: Practices for culturally sustaining classrooms* (pp. 65–93). London: Palgrave Macmillan. https://doi.org/ 10.1007/978-3-030-24788-1

Quijano, A. (2000). Coloniality of power, ethnocentrism, and Latin America. *Nepantla, 1*(3), 533–580.

Smolcic, E., & Katunich, J. (2017). Review article: Teachers crossing borders: A review of the research into cultural immersion field experience for teachers. *Teaching and Teacher Education, 62*, 47–59. https://doi.org/ 10.1016/j.tate.2016.11.002

Suárez-Orozco, C., Abo-Zena, M., & Marks, A. (Eds.). (2015). *Transitions: The development of children of immigrants*. New York, NY: New York University Press.

Walsh, C. (2007). Shifting the geopolitics of critical knowledge: Decolonial thought and cultural studies 'others' in the Andes. *Cultural Studies, 21*(2–3), 224–239.

Conclusion: Building the Loving Community
The Manifesto's Promise

We understand centering the identities of Latinx students in international study programs may at first seem marginal to the entire industry of study abroad. This is precisely why we dared to dream our programs into life and why we have written this book, to bring wisdom of practice from the margins, often located in the Global South, toward the center, often referred to as the Global North. As the United States becomes increasingly Brown and otherwise diverse, it is increasingly reckoning with demographic shifts—even if for little other reason than market pressures that recognize the buying power of Brown communities. Beyond a sense of marketizing Brown dollars that could be thrown at study abroad, we instead draw from the threads of strengths these communities have brought to what is now U.S. soil toward reclaiming strengths for cultural and communal maintenance. We revisit the highlights shared in preceding chapters, provide additional insights about cautions related to this work, and then synthesize lessons by providing a set of recommendations and guiding principles. This is all toward helping build small, loving communities on international study programs who can sow seeds upon return of the loving communities they experience during their programs. In our case, we recognize those who can bring the wealth of the Global South to ailing spaces of the Global North.

Findings Revisited

In Chapter 1, we delved into the current state of study abroad and the necessity to shift the focus from Whiteness to center Latinx and other students of color in education abroad programs. By developing these programs, study abroad faculty foster the strengths of underrepresented students in international immersion programs to be free to be themselves and validate their experiences and beliefs. Specifically, we examined an education abroad experience in ancestral homelands in Mexico. We offer an alternative theoretical perspective toward education abroad programs.

Using a decolonizing lens, Chapter 2 explores the pedagogical and research approaches central to the findings delineated in this book. The findings point to how international program faculty need to deepen the decolonial and relational aspects of the program to draw attention to the quality of the experiences of marginalized students.

In Chapter 3, we described the decolonial pedagogical activities that we planned and engaged in, the reflections and observations of the students and researchers, and the impact that these activities had on the students. We engage the term 'reciprocity' as a decolonial way to construct the relationships between the students and the local people and place. The program's curriculum intentionally confronted inaccuracies learned in school in the Global North so the Latinx students could rewrite what they learned. Throughout the program, the students were unlearning the influence of the dominant culture and collectively learning compassion and collaboration.

The study abroad program was designed for everyone to have their own experience, although Chapter 4 highlights the community building within the group and the opportunity to connect more effectively with people in the local community of Cuernavaca. The decolonizing curriculum provided collaborations with the local community by participating in classes at CILAC-Freire (social justice-oriented language school) and service learning in Caminando Unidos (Indigenously oriented alternative school) along with the homestays. Acknowledging differences, our host partners and students did not view socioeconomic or cultural differences as barriers to forming strong affective connections.

In Chapter 5, we revealed how the Latinx students reconnected with their own internal selves. The flipping of frames and scripts in terms of race and language in the international program context provided new spaces of possibility and deep reflection for the Latinx students and (re)engaged their identity, language skill set, and political consciousness.

Cautionary Notes

Before explaining the basic elements, we recommend the establishment of programs that center Latinx student identities, we turn to some experiences held during other programs as cautionary tales. We offer what we have learned in our decades of experience so that others may avoid the struggles and pitfalls which do not serve the desired objectives of those designing decolonially oriented international study experiences with Latinx students at the center.

If a program has a co-sponsor or a co-director, we recommend they can both communicate openly and share a truly decolonial vision for the program. For instance, I (Kasun) led a program with a school district one summer for their mostly Latinx public school teachers to visit Cuernavaca and Indigenous parts of the state of Veracruz. While much was gained, a Latinx district advisor told me at the U.S.-based orientation that I could no longer discuss the Zapatista movement with the teachers and openly questioned my wisdom about discussing local and global economic conditions. I believe this district leader was worried about what other district partners might have said if they knew the program engaged knowledge about the autonomous and collectivist Zapatista movement or concerns about financial systems. I never dialogued with the director about it, as I suspected the discussion would have escalated tensions in a program that would never be repeated (the funding ended that year independent of my program). Outcomes I experienced included: participants who engaged less with their Latinx heritages and identities than other programs I have run, lower sense of understanding global factors related to identities and oppression, and the participants' relatively lower sense of agency to care about or rectify these oppressions.

We realize there are times when a sponsor provides funds for participants that can seem too hard to pass on. Two of us have taken such funds—solely so less-resourced students can attend our programs—with mixed results. At times, we have found ourselves agreeing to do 'service-learning', a model we sometimes find more patronizing than helpful, even though the request has come from Latinx organizations at times. Despite this conflict, we have felt that we have often been able to still achieve the learning objectives and be in reciprocity with the community by being transparent about funding concerns and if the community members still want to engage in our work. At other times, we have had funders attend our programs and have found the participants to be a resource to engage in dialog and community activities with ganas, sometimes turning into longer-term fruitful professional relationships.

In March 2023, Martha Mata and I (Kaşun) met during one of my work trips to Mexico for a half-day of conversation, program planning, and friendship. Mata told me she hoped she would include some of the following as words of caution, as well, for readers of this text. Mata has received several U.S. groups designated legally as 'Dreamers', those who were granted some legal rights to work in the United States and, in theory, on a pathway to legal citizenship (that still has not come to fruition). She has worked with more than one coordinator, so her words of caution come from more than one difficult experience. She said that it is critical that the participants have some kind of guidelines established about the objectives of the program and that they are held accountable in some way (such as through coursework) to them. She also said that the program coordinator(s) must be someone who is understood as being coherent in word and action (e.g. espousing social justice values and not mistreating the housekeepers at the hotel or outdrinking the students most nights at the bar).

Mata also cautioned that though the group coordinators are Latinx, it does not mean that they will achieve decolonial outcomes, based on her lived experience. She has said she has heard Dreamer participants make negative general comments about Mexico despite their experiences there (and their Latinx coordinators), the kinds of comments she said she has seldom heard from other program participants overall, such as, 'I'm so glad I don't live in this country!' In the meantime, attending to groups of students who overall might seem to not appreciate her school's efforts can have a negative impact on her and her colleagues' sense of mission in their work. We recognize that participants with complex legal statuses certainly have a different set of challenges than those with full legal status to enter and exit their country of citizenship with little trouble. This book's authors agreed that including these cautions was important as a way to honor Mata's work and her wisdom of practice. These words of caution also underscore the reality that this work is not easy or natural, and that it requires thoughtful and purposeful planning. We now turn to that purposefulness in the following section.

In a separate word of caution, we express our anxiety about increased financial pressures in our increasingly neoliberal world. Over the last few decades, we have witnessed that students increasingly have less disposable income and time to attend to university obligations with increased costs of attending college, increased inflation, and lower rates of job stability and pay. All three authors note that we have increasingly struggled over the years with finding ways for students to pay for the programs they attend. As Latinx and BIPOC students tend to come from more limited financial resources, they bear a disproportionate burden related to attending international study programs. Kasun's university, in recognition of this fact and serving a majority of Black, Indigenous, People of Color (BIPOC)) students, offers a $1,000 scholarship (and others) available to the vast majority who complete a very simple application. This helps offset costs.

We recommend understanding the cost structures of the program so that providers in the host country are paid fairly but that overhead be as limited as possible so as not to pass on unnecessary costs to very price-sensitive populations. In the past, I (Kasun) found ways to structure the required university course to meet other program requirements so that students did not also have to pay for an extra course (must universities require that students also take a course, and we note this helps provide the common language and theoretical positioning as well as structured reflection time for the experience). This meant students avoided paying for an extra course. Similarly, finding organizations and institutions that are willing to sponsor specific populations is another way to support students who stand to gain so much. We have had mixed results in these efforts and believe often that it is who one knows and the timing that impacts the results of such queries.

Building a Study Abroad Community

Throughout this book, we have shown the program design and its execution in terms of how the students engaged with the curriculum, the people, the place, and each other. Recognizing our own fraught positioning as hailing from the Global North, we have made our best efforts to center people whose ancestors hail from the Global South, Latinx youth, as the focal point for setting up this program and others like it that we have run. We have attempted to (re)connect them with Global South wisdoms and their heritage language (or at least one of their heritage languages, Spanish). Despite our own Whiteness, we have built our programs in a way where students of color, and, in this case, Latinx students, are clear that the space is theirs for the taking, indeed, a space without Whiteness (Zavala, 2016), one in which they are invited to embody their learning in this respite from something that might feel like total Whiteness throughout the United States. We have called these efforts decolonial (Grande, 2015; Mignolo, 2011; Mohanty, 2003; Quijano, 2000)—and we believe them to be so—in how we have established reciprocal relationships with partners in Mexico that have resulted in friendships and years of bonding. We have found successes in establishing clear parameters with participants and a series of elements we identify and describe in the following section.

We note that these elements are not required in any particular order, but that they all co-constitute each other. For us, these are the key points in creating a decolonial study abroad program where Latinx students are centered on who they are and how they can strengthen and maintain their identities as part of these visits to other Latin American spaces.

We borrow from Indigenous knowledge's orientation toward right relationships (Cajete, 2000; Kimmerer, 2013) and balance with a sense of **reciprocity as founding value and practice**. This means that all our dealings—whether it be with partners in Mexico, the Latinx students, administrators on campus, among ourselves as coordinators—are done with the intention of maintaining harmony and care. We intend to exemplify and embody these values so that our participants also want to share them during (and after) the international study experience. It also aligns heavily with decoloniality and the sense that we can be in right relationship with each other despite the harms provoked from colonization, that we can restore relationships, even, that have been historically fraught, such as the Global South and the Global North. Indeed, our desire to (re)enter the Global South geographically comes from a need for our own healing as well as restoration.

A second element is **centering and creating a decolonial curriculum**. As mentioned previously, the course must center decoloniality, as well as the activities embedded in the experience. This curriculum must also be embodied by the advisors to the best extent possible. Readings should center

110 Conclusion: Building the Loving Community

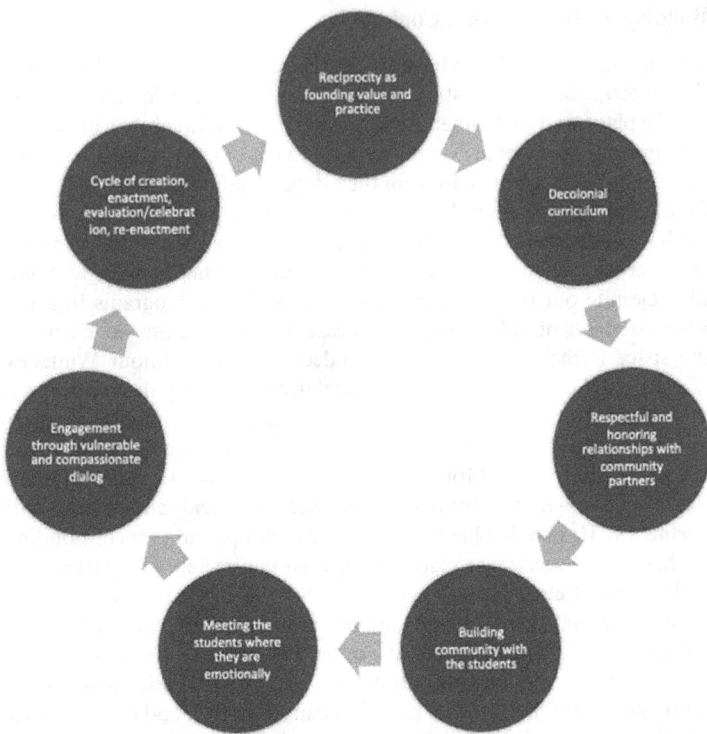

Figure 6.1 Guiding principles of centering Latinx students in study abroad.

thinkers who align with or position themselves in the knowledge of the Global South. Experiences must be tailored from host families who can support this thinking to speakers who also do the same. Visits must also be made through this lens. Touristing is absolutely not the goal. If more traditional spaces are visited that are often for tourists (e.g. global painting phenomenon Frida Kahlo's house), the discussion surrounding the experience, formally, is, 'What was happening that supported social justice struggles; how was Kahlo's life part of this; what do we see in her and her partner's art that points to these struggles?' Working directly with people engaged in decoloniality is ideal—whether it be through a Freirian language school or with a partner on the ground building a new form of community aligned with the Four Agreements (Ruiz, 1997).

The third element we identify is **respectful and honoring relationships with community partners**. This means we are able to be coherent in embodying decolonial values and our reciprocity by acknowledging how much we have to learn from our partners on the ground. It also often points to friendship, which happens naturally when people share values and repeated experiences together. While surely there will be moments of frustration at times, the strength of a years-long relationship allows for elements of trust, sharing, and connection to occur. We note that we as advisors have been profoundly impacted by the hospitality offered to us, and we have taken these elements into our daily lives in the Global North, such as through having convivios upon return and being available for former participants as mentors and even friends.

The fourth element is one of the most dynamic and exciting, if not also at times challenging—**building community with the students**. While no one can force community, a well-grounded advisor can create the conditions so students can feel safety and authenticity in the experiences leading up to departure and how the experiences are had in the host country. This requires multiple informal and formal check-ins where the advisor creates space for the students to talk and reflect. It requires the advisor to push the students into discomfort at the right moments, and not in heavy-handed ways that can create resistance to learning. Knowing the line between these phenomena requires being in touch with the group while not centering on the advisor's own personality as the purpose of the experience. The advisor's best position is as trusted facilitator in this case. The students then are encouraged to really listen to each other and be available as support for each other (and even for the advisor, at times). This sense of community then creates immense space for each individual to have the safety to learn and be open to the complexities of so much of the newness in the host country.

Related closely to the fourth element of community creation requires **meeting the students where they are emotionally**. Over the years, this element has shown its malleability as cultures have shifted. It requires an elasticity and an ability to see past what the advisor might believe is 'right' about her or his ideas of where the students *should* be. It means allowing for the wounds of the past that the students bring individually and collectively to have space to be seen and voiced. It means allowing for students to have the kinds of friendship and spiritual experiences they might have, from trips to churches that might represent their families heritages or the interiors of ancient sweat lodges where their ancestors may also have congregated pre-Conquest. It means understanding that their time constraints are at times genuinely frustratingly limiting in terms of how much the students can prepare prior to departure and allowing for each moment while away to be precious and cherished. This requires a great deal of energy and space on the part of the advisor. The payoffs, however, are enormous. Community building is never guaranteed, but under these conditions is created to greater and lesser extents in the decolonial context of reciprocity.

A key element to establishing this loving community is **engagement through vulnerable and compassionate dialog**, the sixth element. Beyond our postures as experts in our respective fields, with all the protections provided by degrees, certifications, and our formal titles in our institutions is the much more demanding space of expressing real compassion and vulnerability (Brantmeier, 2013; Brown, 2008). To be clear, we are not advocating oversharing, especially over wounds the advisors have not closed to some extent—the experience is not meant for the advisor to do her own emotional processing. Rather, the space is made available for students to have compassion for themselves, each other, and even for the advisors to have their own self-compassion for this complex and demanding work. A host of sources show how challenged students feel in these experiences. The advisor and the community can create ways for students to reflect rapidly about their progress and continue in dynamic growth throughout group reflections and written reflections and in their safe home stays. Partners in the host country are also key to embracing the spirit of this kind of compassion that allows students space to grow (while not allowing, of course, for misbehavior that is mean, arrogant, or ethnocentric).

The final and seventh element we point to is the **overall cycle of creation, enactment, evaluation/celebration, re-enactment**. This means that throughout the experience the students are asked to discuss what has worked best for them, what they might like to change, and certainly when the experience is culminating both celebrating and evaluating. Celebrating is a serious design element—from collective meals held during the experience to a final get-together with music, elaborate food prepared by host families all together, and final words of remembering and sharing. The space can be reclaimed upon return in the form of group chats and collective get-togethers. We know students struggle with how to share the richness of what they learned and how they grew upon return—such group chats and reunions can help maintain a sense of the cause for celebration and continued reflection.

Looking Forward

Based on our work and our recommendations, we close this manifesto. In this one centering of Latinx students in our program, we offer a continued call to bring those from the margins to the center in the construction and consideration of international study programs. The margins include groups that have been left out—wittingly or not—from participation and from decision-making of all matter of curricular experience. Equally important, we recognize the need for all such programming to be framed through lenses of decoloniality. We explore each idea in the following paragraphs in greater detail.

It is said that if anyone is harmed, if anyone is left out, then no one can truly fully belong or enjoy anything that is created and the creation by its nature cannot be done in balance, reciprocity, or harmony. In our efforts to work in harmony, we are well aware that students who have been left out—Black, Indigenous, poor, Latinx, and so on—deserve and need to be at the center of considerations for international study programming. Anything else is the perpetuation of further social inequities. Those who run study abroad programs, then, are tasked with no longer just doing the building of programs for (White) students, but for specifically considering how to make programs be rich experiences that are also safe for other kinds of students. It is worth mentioning the White students who have attended our programs as minorities have often learned a great deal more, it has seemed, than when they have been the vast majority of students on a program.

Specifically, centering the historically marginalized in program construction means conducting outreach to such students; vocalizing and highlighting that the program indeed does center their identities as central to the experience. In actual recruiting, this means including not just faces in photos and images from prior trips, but including information about *how* such students are centered in ways that also does not make the students feel like they are being called out. The kinds of comments we have used have included how we center decolonial thought, equity, and justice as part of our programming, which means valuing the students who attend and saying out loud the backgrounds of students we have worked with. It also means explaining that a chief goal of the experience is creating a community where people are valued and allowed to be who they are without silencing what has been historically forced to be left out of discussions. It also requires outreach to organizations that work with historically marginalized students.

We also recognize that creating a version of 'study abroad' that meant something like tourism with a twist is no longer acceptable. Thus, we center the decolonial as the goal and foundation of the work we do to undergird the entire experience, and especially the curriculum, as the curriculum is the shared common glue of the group. Readings, then, must reflect this decolonial aspiration, as must discussions within the group. This means the group leader/facilitator/faculty member must be coherent in their efforts to also live such decoloniality, for how can students otherwise learn but through example? As the world continues to be a place of creation and reciprocity among many creatures, it is also a place that finds itself in increasing crises. Failing to recognize these crises and act as if the decolonial weren't a necessity, a true urgency, is, at best, folly, and, at worst, willful ignorance. Similarly, we hope to see a continued growth in the still minimal (though growing) scholarship surrounding study abroad and students of color. We are steadfast in our understanding of how powerful international study experiences can be for transformation, for community building, and for creating loving communities, and we offer this text as a key piece in creating those efforts.

References

Brantmeier, E. J. (2013). Pedagogy of vulnerability: Definitions, assumptions and applications. In J. Lin, R.L. Oxford, & E. J. Brantmeier (Eds.), *Re-envisioning higher education: Embodied pathways to wisdom and social transformation* (pp. 96–106). Information Age.

Brown, B. (2008). *I thought it was just me (but it isn't): Making the journey from "What will people think" to "I am enough"*. New York: Avery.

Cajete, G. (2000). Indigenous knowledge: The pueblo metaphor of indigenous education. In M. Battiste (Ed.), *Reclaiming indigenous voice and vision* (pp. 181–191). Vancouver, Canada: UBC Press.

Grande, S. (2015). *Red pedagogy: Native American social and political thought* (10th ed.). Lanham, Maryland: Rowman & Littlefield.

Kimmerer, R. (2013). *Braiding sweetgrass: Indigenous wisdom, scientific knowledge, and the teachings of plants*. Canada: Milkweed Editions.

Mignolo, W. (2011). *The darker side of western modernity: Global futures, decolonial options*. Durham, NC: Duke University Press.

Mohanty, C. T. (2003). *Feminism without borders: Decolonizing theory, practicing solidarity*. Durham, NC: Duke University Press.

Quijano, A. (2000). Coloniality of power, ethnocentrism, and Latin America. *Nepantla, 1*(3), 533–580.

Ruiz, D. M. (1997). *The four agreements: A Toltec wisdom book*. San Rafael, CA: Amber-Allen.

Zavala, M. (2016). Design, participation, and social change: What design in grassroots spaces can teach learning scientists. *Cognition & Instruction, 34*(3), 236–249.

Index

Activist 35–36, 39, 68, 71, 74, 76–77, 82, 92, 95–96
agency 2, 11, 40, 50, 54, 57, 69–70, 89, 107
ancestors 51, 53–54, 109, 111
Anzaldúa, Gloria 14, 52, 71, 93

Blackwell, Kelsey 6, 10, 29
blanqueamiento 6
building relationships 63–67

Caminando Unidos 39, 59, 68–71, 78–87, 106
Cautionary notes 106
Ceremony 52, 76
CILAC Freire vi, 31, 31–34, 39, 52, 54, 65–67, 69–78, 81–95, 106
Class discussions 36–42, 55, 60, 65, 77, 79, 95, 101
Collaboration 70–75, 106
colonial era 2, 10
Colonization 1, 3, 7, 15, 19, 51, 69–71, 89–97, 102, 109
Community 3–14, 17–21, 28, 32, 35–46, 49–67, 69–87, 89–102, 105–114
compassion 10, 43, 50, 61–67, 81, 86, 106, 112
Connections 13, 30–43, 51–54, 63–67, 69–87, 92, 94, 98, 106
Consciousness 1, 10, 19, 46, 54, 67, 70–74, 89–106
Convivencia 81
Critical ethnographic case study 39–41
Cuernavaca 1, 7, 31–41, 72–87, 90–95, 106
Curriculum 1, 3, 18, 28, 54–57, 69–71, 91, 95, 106, 113

Data analysis 44–45
Decolonial curriculum 36, 78, 109
Decolonization 14–19, 41–44, 95
Decolonizing study abroad 14–17
Dialogue 13, 36–44, 55, 72, 75
Disappeared 35, 37, 75, 94–95
Dreamers vi, 32, 74, 107

Education abroad 1–3, 10–12, 28, 99, 105
Esteva, Gustavo 1, 4, 17, 78, 96
Ethics 45–46
Ethnic studies 3
Evaluation 76

feminism 51, 57
Four agreements 36–39, 42–43, 58, 60–61
Freire 75, 83

Global North/ Global South 11, 14–18, 40–41, 54, 57–80, 89, 91–102, 105–111
Guiding principles for building study abroad 106–114

Healing 1–8, 10, 18–19, 29, 37–38, 52–53, 61–63, 72, 109
hegemony of English 7
heritage speakers 19
Heritage study 24, 32
Homestay families 33–35, 41–45, 70–76, 81–86, 90
Homestays 33, 69, 81, 83, 106

Identity 40–43, 55, 62, 71, 80, 83, 89–106
Illich, Ivan 35

Index

Indigeneity 15
interconnectedness 13
Interviews 29, 34, 40–43, 70

Jefferies, Julián vi, 24, 30, 32

Kasun, G. Sue 1, 4–7, 18–24, 29–46, 49, 52, 55–66, 74–78, 101, 106–108
Kimmerer 16, 50, 109

Land 15–16, 35, 51, 62, 96
Language 1–2, 5, 7, 12, 15, 19, 31–46, 51, 57, 60, 66, 69–87, 89–102, 106–110
Local partners 69–87
Loving community 105–114

Marginalized students 11, 46, 106, 113
Marks, Beth 5, 19, 20–23, 34–38, 41–43, 53, 59, 72, 84
Mata, Martha 31–33, 52, 72, 74–75, 82, 107–108
Mexico City 31, 34–36, 62, 89–90
Mignolo 13–17, 91, 95–96
Mother tongue maintenance 89–102

new tribalism 51–52

Participant observation 29, 41–42
Partnerships 8, 28, 69
Pedagogical strategies 49–67
pobrecito 55–56
Political consciousness 80, 89–102, 106
Positionality 7, 18, 23–24
program planning 29–31, 107

Race 5, 84, 99, 102, 106
Racism 14, 85
Reciprocity 85–87, 106–113
recruiting 28, 30–31, 113

Relationships 8, 16–18, 23, 30–67, 69–102, 106–110
Research design 41–46
Research methodology 39–41
ritual 37–38, 52–54, 62, 85
Ruíz, Don Miguel 36–37

Self-compassion 10, 61–63, 112
Service learning 18–19, 43, 69–102, 106–107
Settler colonialism 15–16
sexuality 22, 33, 65, 84
solidaridad 2
Solidarity 32, 39–40, 45, 57, 69–87
Spanglish 90–94
Spanish 3–5, 7, 19, 23, 34, 36, 40, 42, 49–51, 60, 66, 76–77, 81, 89–102, 109
Storytelling 54
Students of color in study abroad 11–13

Temazcal 38, 52–54, 62–63
Teotihuacan 57, 66
Tepoztlan 61–62, 82
Testimonio 54
Torres, Jorge vi, 32–34, 75
Trustworthiness 45

Valenzuela, Angela 5
Vulnerability 65–67, 112

Ways of knowing 14–24, 37–39, 43, 64
White students in study abroad 3, 6, 10–14, 19, 23, 29, 113
Whiteness 1–8, 10, 18, 29, 51, 89, 105, 109

Zapata 1
Zapatista 1, 33, 39, 76, 96, 107
Zavala, Miguel 2, 3, 7, 10, 19, 109

For Product Safety Concerns and Information please contact our EU representative GPSR@taylorandfrancis.com
Taylor & Francis Verlag GmbH, Kaufingerstraße 24, 80331 München, Germany

www.ingramcontent.com/pod-product-compliance
Lightning Source LLC
Chambersburg PA
CBHW071512150426
43191CB00009B/1494